THE DA VINCI CON

THE GREAT DECEPTION

21ST CENTURY PRESS
PUBLISHING WITH PURPOSE

The Da Vinci Con

Copyright © 2006 By Doug Stauffer

Published by 21st Century Press
2131 W. Republic Rd.
PMB 41
Springfield, MO 65807

All rights reserved. No portion of this book may be reproduced in any form without written permission, except in the case of brief quotations embodied in critical articles or reviews.

For more information about 21st Century Press visit our web site:
www.21stcenturypress.com

ISBN 0-9771964-8-8

Cover Design: Keith Locke
Book Design: Terry White

This book is dedicated to people of faith who do not like their aesthetical pleasures distorted.

Acknowledgements

The author would like to express his deepest appreciation to the following:

Most preeminently, the precious Lord Jesus Christ for His saving and sustaining grace. We are told "...that in all things he might have the preeminence" (Colossians 1:18).

My devoted helpmeet Judy for her support, encouragement, and understanding through our years of marriage and ministry together. Justin and Heather for unselfishly sharing their Dad once again with those in search of truth.

My parents, Richard and Marianne Stauffer, who instilled in me the work ethic and fortitude to never quit. Thank you for the character-building foundation that the Lord used to convict and convince me to repent of my sins and accept the one and only Saviour almost three decades ago.

Miss Michelle Goree for her proofreading and grammatical suggestions. May the Lord bless you for your hard work and dedication and keep you healthy. May the reader take your name boldly before the throne of grace in prayer.

Table of Contents

Chapter 1
Dismantling the Da Vinci Con 9

Chapter 2
Separating Fact from Fiction 21

Chapter 3
Complete Disregard of Faith 29

Chapter 4
Patriarchal vs. Matriarchal Religion 45

Chapter 5
Messiah or Mere Mortal 57

Chapter 6
Marriage of Jesus and Mary Magdalene 63

Chapter 7
Interpreting the Madonna of the Rocks 71

Chapter 8
Who was Mary Magdalene? 75

Chapter 9
A Novel Celebrating Gross Immorality 83

Chapter 10
The Shirley MacLaine Connection 99

Chapter 11
Overview: Mary Magdalene & Gnostic Gospels 103

Chapter 12
Original Sin 107

Addendum 111

1
Dismantling the Da Vinci Con

Proof of the Anti-Christian Nature of the Da Vinci Code

We are in the middle of a war, one that has been going on forever ...to protect the secret so powerful that if revealed, it would devastate the very foundations of mankind ...witness the biggest cover-up in human history.[1]

So goes the provocative trailer for *The Da Vinci Code* movie. The trailer ends with the words **"Seek the *truth*"** flashing on screen. Far from causing the moviegoer to seek and find the truth, this production attacks the authority of God's word, the integrity of the person of Christ and the legitimacy of the entire Christian message. The book inspires a return to the roots of ancient paganism and serves as a camouflaged assault upon Christianity. Dr. Ed Hindson provides these insightful comments:

> The feminization of God is making radical strides in today's popular culture...some have attempted to deify Mary, the earthly mother of Jesus, over the centuries. But now, the shift is to Mary Magdalene...Books like *The Da Vinci Code* prey upon a biblically illiterate generation that loves conspiracy theories and distrusts authority. [2]

Many people are being duped into questioning and

---

[1] Dialog for *The Da Vinci Code* movie trailer (www.ivillage.com).
[2] Dr. Edward Hindson, National Liberty Journal, "Is God a Woman?" pgs. 1, 22.

rejecting the truths which hold the only hope for their lives and souls. This devious assault upon Christianity by *The Da Vinci Code* evokes questions such as the following:

- Is it true that the Bible is false and does not tell us the true story about Jesus?
- Was Jesus really married to Mary Magdalene?
- Are Mary Magdalene and her offspring really the Holy Grail?[3]
- Did Jesus really designate her as the future leader of Christianity?
- Did Leonardo da Vinci really use his art to hide secret codes about the Holy Grail—Mary Magdalene?

The answer to all five questions is a resounding "no." The most dangerous aspect of *The Da Vinci Code* is the fact that the book raises these questions and then answers them by presenting information in a factual setting without one shred of evidence. Dan Brown affirms everything he believes through his characters. He uses supposedly credible historians and other fictional researchers to reinforce his potent myth. These elements, combined with a world-wide conspiracy to debunk the truth of Christ, produces a novel which can influence people down a satanic path of no return.

Dan Brown promulgates intelligent-sounding "evidence" on most every page. The reader is left wondering which tidbit of information is fact and which is fiction. Some will cry out, "The book is only a work of fiction—what's the big deal?" The

---

[3] The Holy Grail or so-called chalice of the Last Supper is mostly folklore and religious mythology. The legends abound for the so-called Holy Grail. Some people claim it to be a beautiful jeweled vessel that can bestow unlimited food and drink upon the bearer. It is also claimed to be the chalice of the Last Supper and the vessel used by Joseph of Arimathea to collect Jesus' blood while on the cross.

problem is that the reading public has accepted many of the assertions made by Dan Brown as fact. Now, the movie going public likewise has the unfortunate opportunity to embrace these false assertions.

Truth is not simply a matter of opinion; truth is truth regardless of who accepts it and who rejects it. Whether truth is placed in a fictional or non-fictional setting is irrelevant. In fact, deception is easier through the medium of fiction since the author can resort to the *fiction excuse* as an out for shoddy research. Dan Brown appears to be a novelist with an agenda, skewing the truth even in his interpretation of proven fact.

Although the work is dubbed fictional, the author would have his readers and the general public to believe otherwise. For instance, on his website, Dan Brown explains how this novel empowers women. He claims to be uncovering lost history—suppressed for thousands of years:

> Two thousand years ago, we lived in a world of Gods and Goddesses. Today, we live in a world solely of Gods. Women in most cultures have been stripped of their spiritual power. The novel touches on questions of how and why this shift occurred...and on what lessons we might learn from it regarding our future.[4]

The reviewers of his novel seem to agree with Brown. *The Da Vinci Code* has been hailed by Janet Maslin of *The New York Times* as "Blockbuster perfection. An exhilaratingly brainy thriller." The *Chicago Tribune* wrote that the book transmits "several doctorates' worth of fascinating history and learned speculation." *The Rocky Mountain News* says it "is that rare book that manages to both entertain and educate simultaneously. ...There is enough medieval history to please any historian...," *Bookpage* says that "Brown's scholarship never slows

---

[4] http://www.danbrown.com/novels/davinci_code/faqs.html

down the sizzling action." There are many other high accolades for this novel on Dan Brown's website, most of them asserting the work's factuality.[5]

The State of the Churches

Dan Brown's novel serves as a propaganda piece for a completely new religious worldview. He simply taps into humanity's deviant search for answers by presenting a preposterous and yet easily believable lie. Satan simply works behind the scenes subtly seducing and deceiving those easily caught up in the hype. There is no doubt that what we think, how we behave and what we believe is influenced by these seemingly innocent lies.

In a nutshell, *The Da Vinci Code* is a reader-friendly denial of the tenets of Christianity. Dan Brown's view of church history revolves almost exclusively around the Roman Catholic institution. He seems to consider all non-Catholic churches as having originated from the Protestant Reformation—an interesting supposition. He fails to account for Christians persecuted prior to the Protestant Reformation, who remained underground for fear of losing their heads.

It is true that many churches today have effectively been derailed from their ultimate purpose of evangelizing the lost. Many people ignorantly proclaim that this transformation has been progressive when in fact Christianity finds itself in a crisis mode. The influences bombarding believers from every direction are taking their toll. The world has radical new views today on morals, the family and religion. Historical ignorance and turning a blind eye toward the present metamorphosis have caused many churches to lose their historical compass. *The Da Vinci Code* is not Dan Brown's first conspiracy book, but builds upon its predecessor.

---

[5] http://www.danbrown.com/novels/davinci_code/reviews.html

Angels and Demons

Brown also included the character Robert Langdon in his previous novel, *Angels and Demons*. In that work, Brown reveals his true religion and thoughts concerning the ideal church. Langdon works alongside Vittoria Vetra when the subject of faith surfaces. Vittoria tells Langdon:

> "Faith is universal. Our specific methods for understanding it are arbitrary. Some of us pray to Jesus, some of us go to Mecca, some of us study subatomic particles. In the end we are all searching for truth, that which is greater than ourselves." Langdon wished that his students could express themselves so dearly.[6]

Brown is correct concerning everyone's search for truth. However, he seems not to realize that truth will not be found by taking a pilgrimage to Mecca or by applying the scientific method. Truth comes from believing the one Book that Brown accomplishes to undermine—the Bible. Brown's unwise thoughts come through quite clearly; he believes that all "faiths" are to be accepted, regardless of the tenets they espouse.

The Storyline

The Da Vinci Code opens with the grisly murder of the Louvre's curator. The crime unites hero Robert Langdon, a professor of religious symbology[7] at Harvard University, with the victim's granddaughter, a police cryptologist named Sophie Neveu. These two figures along with Leigh Teabing, a crippled millionaire historian, attempt to unravel clues to the murder and a deeper plot found in the art of Leonardo da Vinci.

---

[6] Dan Brown, *Angels and Demons*, (New York: Pocket Books, 2000) p. 110.

[7] A non-existent field of study.

Jacques Saunière, the museum's curator, dies protecting the location and identity of the "Holy Grail." Before his death he has enough time to leave various clues—including arranging his body on the floor to form Leonardo da Vinci's *Vitruvian Man*. The *Vitruvian Man* is a famous drawing with accompanying notes that depicts a naked male figure in two superimposed positions. The five points touching the outer circle form a pentagram which is a favored symbol of the Wiccan religion and used in many neo-pagan rituals.[8]

Eventually, Langdon and Sophie are forced to flee Paris for London, staying one step ahead of the police. Of course, there is also a mad albino Opus Dei[9] monk named Silas who will stop at nothing to prevent them from finding the "Holy Grail." This is the gist of the book. But the premise of *The Da Vinci Code* revolves around a centuries-old Vatican grand conspiracy of the alleged marriage of Jesus Christ to Mary Magdalene.

In this blasphemous book, Dan Brown claims that Mary Magdalene is the true *Holy Grail* and their offspring are the royal bloodline. It also offers a new spirituality while portraying Christianity as being based on a big lie (the Deity of Christ) used by patriarchal oppressors to deny the true worship of the Divine Feminine. That is, according to Brown, true historical spirituality balanced both male and female

---

[8] The pentagram was also used by Aleister Crowley, Anton LaVey (author of *The Satanic Bible*), the masons and witchcraft. The inclusion of the ram's head signifies Baphomet—a demonic deity and symbolic of Satan.

[9] Opus Dei began in 1928 and currently has 86,000 members. This sect believes in physical mortification by whipping themselves with a knotted rope and by wearing a cilice—a spiked chain worn around the thigh. The secrecy surrounding the group encourages speculation. They publish no membership list and discourage members from announcing their membership in the organization.

components, such that goddesses and the power of women were revered.

According to the plot of the book, Jesus supposedly marries Mary Magdalene and entrusts the leadership of His movement to her. She is pregnant with His child when He is (or is not) crucified. The other apostles are jealous of her position and suppress the truth causing Mary Magdalene to flee to Paris, France where her offspring become the root of the royal Merovingian line.

The Knights Templar and the Priory of Sion are the protectors of the truth and of the royal bloodline (or Holy Grail). Saunière and his granddaughter Sophie are of the Merovingian line. Sophie is unaware of this fact and has distanced herself from her grandfather after witnessing him in a secret room in his country home engaging in some form of ritualistic sex before a crowd of masked, chanting onlookers.

The reader finally learns that Mary Magdalene's remains and the documents proving the royal bloodline are buried within I.M. Pei's glittering, glass, seventy-foot pyramid at the entrance of the Louvre. At the end of the novel, Langdon falls down to this knees in reverence to this "holy" place and "hears" the wisdom of the ages in a woman's voice speaking to him.

> Like the murmurs of spirits in the darkness, forgotten words echoed. *The quest for the Holy Grail is the quest to kneel before the bones of Mary Magdalene. A journey to pray at the feet of the outcast one.* With a sudden upwelling of reverence, Robert Langdon fell to his knees. For a moment, he thought he heard a woman's voice...the wisdom of ages...whispering up from the chasms of earth. (emphasis in original)[10]

---

[10] Dan Brown, *The Da Vinci Code* (New York: Doubleday, 2003), p. 454—Epilogue.

Background

This book is simply an offshoot of the 1982 book *Holy Blood, Holy Grail* by Richard Leigh. It has been described as a *"radical new view of Christianity's origins."* It is in fact an updated rendition of other similar irreverent works that simply engross the reader and carry him down a conspiratorial path and spiritual journey. With a little research, the literary deficiencies and inaccuracies within the work are easily recognizable. A first year Bible college student could easily pinpoint the blasphemous content.

The book corresponds in many ways to a blasphemous movie produced in 1988 by Martin Scorsese entitled *The Last Temptation of Christ*. This movie also depicted Jesus as having sex with Mary Magdalene. In Dan Brown's book, the offspring of the alleged relationship—Sarah—is to be the true heir to the kingdom.

The deeper subplot of *The Da Vinci Code* shows that the truth of the sacred feminine has now immerged from the shadows of the past having been kept secret from the public at large. Like the Priory of Sion, the new holders of the secret are waiting for the "right time in history to share their secret. A time when the world is ready to handle the truth."[11] This approach sounds similar to the Bible's timetable concerning Satan. He will reveal to the world his plan and design during "the hour of temptation."[12] The world will unsuspectingly swallow the lie until it is eternally too late. Because the world will believe his lie, the Bible prophesies that "all the world wondered after the beast."[13] *The Da Vinci Code* joins a long list of influences preparing the world for the lie that they will all one day believe.

---

[11] Brown, p. 295.
[12] Revelation 3:10.
[13] Revelation 13:3.

A Work of Fiction

From the outset, I want to make it clear that I am fully aware that this book is a work of fiction, but a dangerous one. Dan Brown disregards the premise of "historical fiction" which is the act of portraying history using fictional characters. Regardless of his bold claims to historical accuracy, he misinterprets and misrepresents history and theology. Sadly, most people are not adequately equipped to discern fact from fiction and generally absorb as truth that which is most preposterous.

The book has been shown to be based on fraudulent manuscripts and poor scholarship. Brown is guilty of sheer revisionism and both subtly and overtly attacks the very foundations of Christianity. Laura Miller of the *New York Times* describes the book as a work of "pop pseudohistory." She continues, "What seems increasingly clear...is that 'The Da Vinci Code,' like 'Holy Blood, Holy Grail,' is based on a notorious hoax...Dozens of credible details are heaped up in order to provide a legitimizing cushion for rank nonsense." [14]

The Da Vinci Code will not shake the faith of any well grounded believer. However, worshippers of Jesus Christ and preachers of the Gospel have the responsibility to sound the alarm for unbelievers and those weaker in the faith. Brown's book and the media hype surrounding it have the potential to cause men and women to view the Bible as simply a pack of lies. Any work, whether fiction or not, must be closely scrutinized when its intended purpose is to distort the truth.

Religious leaders increasingly call for the unity of all faiths—with the exception of true biblical Christianity. The world is looking for a global religious unity in hopes that this will bring peace. America's new calling seems to be to lead the

---

[14] Laura Miller, "The Last Word; The Da Vinci Con," *The New York Times*, February 22, 2004. http://query.nytimes.com/gst/fullpage.html?res=9B07E0DD103AF931A15751C0A9629C8B63

way in developing a unified spirituality. Dan Brown extols the virtues of a type of pre-Christian pagan spirituality. However, he must first attempt to destroy the one thing holding back this world-wide union—the teaching that Jesus Christ was the one true God manifest in human form. As such, He is the only One that qualifies for our worship and adoration.

The Attack on the Deity of Jesus Christ

A fundamental teaching of the Bible revolves around the Deity of Jesus Christ—the teaching that God was manifest in human form. If Jesus is simply a mere mortal and not God, the whole Bible crumbles to pieces as does Christianity. Here are a few quotes from *The Da Vinci Code* that reveal Brown's attack on the Deity of Jesus Christ.

> ...Jesus was viewed by his followers as a mortal prophet... a great and powerful man, but a man nonetheless. A mortal. [15]

> ...Constantine upgraded Jesus' status almost four centuries **after** Jesus' death, thousands of documents already existed chronicling His life as a **mortal** man. [16]

> ...almost everything our fathers taught us about Christ is **false**. [17]

> ...the greatest story ever told is, in fact, the greatest story ever **sold**. [18]

Most people recognize that the "greatest story ever told"

---

[15] Brown, p. 233.
[16] Ibid., p. 234.
[17] Ibid., p. 235.
[18] Ibid., p. 267.

refers to Christ and His teachings. Dan Brown's book unapologetically and boldly attacks the Deity of Christ and His word. Brown attacks Christ while claiming that the book is not anti-Christian.

On Dan Brown's website, he answers *Frequently Asked Questions*. The third question reads: **"Is this book anti-Christian?"** Of course, he answers no.[19] Dozens of quotes are provided herein taken directly from his book to unequivocally disprove his assertion that *The Da Vinci Code* is not anti-Christian.

Another question, further down the page on his website asks, **"Are you a Christian?"** His answer: *"Yes. Interestingly, if you ask three people what it means to be Christian, you will get three different answers. Some feel being baptized is sufficient. Others feel you must accept the Bible as absolute historical fact. Still others require a belief that all those who do not accept Christ as their personal savior are doomed to hell. Faith is a continuum, and we each fall on that line where we may."* [20]

These personal statements reveal Dan Brown's confused state. Whether or not a person is a Christian is not a matter of one's own opinion or viewpoint. The Bible determines the truth of the matter, not Dan Brown or any other human being. As Brown continues to defend what he has written, it is hard to believe he is truly a Christian.

His influence cannot be underestimated. The book spent fifteen weeks as the #1 best seller on the *New York Times* bestseller list. It has sold over 40 million copies in 44 languages worldwide. Solely because of this book, *Time* magazine named Dan Brown one of the world's 100 most influential people in April 2005.[21] Should a writer who uses his position to influence so many others simply be disregarded as irrelevant?

---

[19] http://www.danbrown.com/novels/davinci_code/faqs.html
[20] http://www.danbrown.com/novels/davinci_code/faqs.html
[21] *Time,* April 11, 2005, "The Novel that Ate the World,"
http://www.danbrown.com/media/morenews/time041505.htm
http://www.time.com/time/press_release/article/0,8599,1047355,00.htm

2
Separating Fact from Fiction

Dan Brown does not believe that he is simply making up a plotline. He maintains that his story is based on fact. Matt Lauer of "The Today Show" interviewed Dan Brown and asked him about the historical accuracy of the book: *"How much is this based on reality in terms of things that actually occurred?"*

Dan Brown's absurd response: *"Absolutely all of it. Obviously, ...Robert Langdon is fictional, but all of the art, architecture, secret rituals, secret societies, all of that is historical fact."*[22]

Dan Brown claims that his book is based on historical fact. His writing style subtly causes the reader to trust in the credibility of the dialog by including fictional experts with impeccable credentials. Most people do not have the scholarly wherewithal to determine where these "reputable historians" err. Interestingly, the thoughts of Dan Brown's characters are really his own thoughts articulated in a manner similar to the mouthpiece of a puppet. Dan Brown admits as much in his *Good Morning America* interview of November 3, 2003.

> I began the research for *The Da Vinci Code* as a skeptic. I entirely expected, as I researched the book, to disprove this theory. And after numerous trips to Europe, about two years of research, I really became a believer. And it's important to remember that this is a novel about a theory that has been out there for a long time.

It is comical for Brown to claim that just because something has existed for "a long time" that it becomes any more

---

[22] *The Today Show, NBC*, June 9, 2003, Dan Brown interview by Matt Lauer. http://www.danbrown.com/media/todayshow.htm

than a theory. The whole foundation for the accuracy and creditability of *The Da Vinci Code* is based on the existence of an organization called the Priory of Sion. The Priory of Sion never existed in the form or at least for the reason that Brown suggests. This organization ceased to exist in the early 1600's and was hijacked in the early 1900's by an anti-Semitic occultist who admired Adolf Hitler. Brown's facts are a flimsy fabrication easily refuted by the evidence.

The Priory of Sion

Dan Brown claims that the Priory of Sion in his book is the original organization founded nine centuries ago. He begins his book with a prefatory list of "facts." On the very first page, he writes:

> FACT: The Priory of Sion—a European secret society founded in 1099—is a real organization. [23]

The book claims that ***the Priory of Sion*** guards the secret of Jesus' marriage to Mary Magdalene and watches and protects Jesus and Mary's supposed descendants from that marriage. However, things are not as they seem. The organizational name mentioned in Brown's book was hijacked from the original Priory of Sion which was a Catholic priory of monks that existed from about 1100 until 1617.

The parchments used to prove the authenticity of the Priory of Sion have been proven to be completely bogus. They were planted in the French National Library in Paris. A Frenchman named Pierre Plantard (1920-2000) made his living by working as a paid sexton in the Catholic Church of Saint-Louis d'Antin. On May 7, 1956, he founded a political social club named ***The Priory of Sion***, also known as C.I.R.C.U.I.T.—(*Chivalry of Catholic Rule and Institution and of*

---

[23] Brown, p. 1.

Independent Traditionalist Union). The same year that he founded the Priory of Sion, Plantard spent a year in jail (1956-1957) for abuse of minors and was subsequently divorced from his wife.

Throughout the next two decades, Plantard fabricated documents about the Priory of Sion which purportedly proved the Jesus-Mary Magdalene theory and that the true French royalty (the Merovingians)[24] were their descendants. Plantard claimed that he was a living descendant of this family and true heir to the throne, making him also a living descendent of Jesus Christ and Mary Magdalene! Dan Brown must have fallen for Plantard's deceptive tactics because he includes Plantard in his book when he states that there are only two family bloodlines remaining.

> Only two direct lines of Merovingians remain. Their family names are Plantard and Saint-Clair. Both families live in hiding, probably protected by the Priory. [25]

Plantard also claimed that the Priory of Sion, which he founded in 1956, was the much older organization dating back to 1099. Both the BBC and the History Channel have produced programs which prove that Plantard registered the Priory of Sion in 1956. [26]

Plantard Exposed

A BBC special and several French books document a lawsuit involving a friend of the French president. During the court proceedings, Plantard testifies under oath that the documents about Jesus and Mary Magdalene were false and that he, Philippe de Chérisey and Gérard de Sède fabricated the

---

[24] The Merovingians are also mentioned in two of the Matrix movies
[25] Brown, p. 260.
[26] Di Massimo Introvigne, "Beyond 'The Da Vinci Code': What is the Priory of Sion?" Center for Studies on New Religions. http://www.cesnur.org/2004/mi_davinci_en.htm

entire matter. Yet, these are the very documents which form the premise for Brown's *Da Vinci Code* book. [27]

The Priory of Sion referred to in the book did not begin in 1099 as claimed, but in 1956. The underlying documents are falsified; therefore, the whole book is a farce. Laura Miller, writing for *The New York Times,* summarizes the hoax of Plantard, the Priory of Sion and the Merovingians as follows:

> Finally, though, the legitimacy of the Priory of Sion history rests on a cache of clippings and pseudonymous documents that even the authors of "Holy Blood, Holy Grail" suggest were planted in the Bibliothèque Nationale by a man named Pierre Plantard. As early as the 1970's, one of Plantard's confederates had admitted to helping him fabricate the materials, including genealogical tables portraying Plantard as a descendant of the Merovingians (and, presumably, of Jesus Christ) and a list of the Priory's past "grand masters." This patently silly catalog of intellectual celebrities includes Botticelli, Isaac Newton, Jean Cocteau and, of course, Leonardo da Vinci. Furthermore, this is the same list that Dan Brown trumpets as fact, along with the alleged nine-century pedigree of the Priory, in *The Da Vinci Code*. Plantard, it is eventually revealed, was an inveterate rascal with a criminal record for fraud and affiliations with wartime anti-Semitic and right-wing groups. The actual Priory of Sion was a tiny, harmless group of like-minded friends formed in 1956. [28]

---

[27] Documented in James Garlow and Peter Jones, *Cracking Da Vinci's Code* (Colorado Springs, CO: Cook Communications, 2004), p. 112.
[28] Laura Miller.

The Point of the Book

Dan Brown communicates the point of the whole book when he mentions the worship of Mary Magdalene.

> The Priory of Sion, to this day, still worships Mary Magdalene as the Goddess, the Holy Grail, the Rose, and the Divine Mother. [29]

This religion is no different than all of the other religions with their female deities. The mastermind behind all of this confusion is none other than Satan himself. He wants to steal the worship that rightfully belongs to our Saviour Jesus Christ. Any teaching that accomplishes this is antichrist.

True Worshippers

Everything about one's spiritual worship is important. Christianity is demonstrably unique and God the Father is seeking those that will worship Him in spirit and in truth.

> But the hour cometh, and now is, when the true worshippers shall worship the Father in spirit and in truth: for **the Father seeketh such to worship him.** God is a Spirit: and **they that worship him must worship him in spirit and in truth.** [30]

The Anti-Christ, the Beast, will convince all those whose names are not written in the Book of Life to worship him instead of God.

> **And all that dwell upon the earth shall worship him**, whose names are not written in the book of life of the Lamb slain from the foundation of the world.[31]

---

[29] Brown, p. 255.
[30] John 4:23-24.
[31] Revelation 13:8.

God will go to extraordinary lengths in response to Satan's increased efforts to confuse, confound and condemn those that listen to him. During that time God will have one of His angels fly through the air proclaiming that earth's inhabitants are to worship God only.

> Saying with a loud voice, Fear God, and give glory to him; for the hour of his judgment is come: and **worship him** that made heaven, and earth, and the sea, and the fountains of waters. [32]

There are many interrelated influences attempting to prepare the world for the time to come. Each of them accomplishes its goal by drawing people's attention away from the truth. Interestingly, there is a revealing connection between *Harry Potter* and *The Da Vinci Code*. The association between these two books and the Mark of the Beast is both eye opening and uncanny.

Harry Potter and *The Da Vinci Code* Connection

Plantard claimed that the list of Grand Masters of the Priory of Sion included certain *alchemists*. One of these alchemists was **Nicolas Flamel**. Flamel was in fact born in 1330 and died in 1418. Interestingly, the *Harry Potter* books mentioned Flamel as the one who provided his followers with eternal life. It also discretely links him with the Mark of the Beast. Here is how.

Harry Potter and the Philosopher's Stone, first published in Britain in 1997, mentions that Nicolas Flamel had "celebrated his 665 birthday" the preceding year, thus making him 666 in the year in question. When 666 is added to Flamel's birth year of 1330 the result is 1996—the year that the first Harry Potter book was written by J.K. Rowling. According to

---

[32] Revelation 14:7.

the *Harry Potter* material, Flamel has the *elixir of life* which gives a person eternal life. [33]

The *elixir of life* or the Philosopher's Stone was said to be a substance that had the power to transmute base metal into gold. It was also *"a substance thought capable of regenerating a man spiritually."*[34] The problem arises when eternal life is equated with the Mark of the Beast and not a personal relationship with Jesus Christ. Flamel's association with *Harry Potter*, the *Da Vinci Code*, 666 and eternal life is very disturbing. J.K. Rowling and Dan Brown seem to have a common inspirational source and it certainly is not heavenly.

The Truth Concerning the Early Church

Truth mixed cleverly with error has much greater potential for deception than error alone, thus the great danger posed by Brown's book. Another false premise of Dan Brown relates to the author of history:

> ...history is always written by the winners. When two cultures clash, the loser is obliterated, and the winner writes the history books—books which glorify their own cause and disparage the conquered foe. [35]

Truly enough, at times, history has been penned by the victors. However, early Christians were certainly not the victors in the sense intended by Brown.

---

[33] http://www.answers.com/main/ntquery;jsessionid=1crcl3h61ykz2?method=4&dsid=2222&dekey=Dates+in+Harry+Potter&gwp=8&curtab=2222_1&sbid=lc04a&linktext=here

[34] http://www.answers.com/main/ntquery?method=4&dsid=2222&dekey=Philosopher%27s+stone&gwp=8&curtab=2222_1&linktext=philosopher's%20stone

[35] Brown, p. 256.

> But thanks be to **God, which giveth us the victory** through our Lord Jesus Christ.[36]

Although Christians have victory through our Lord Jesus Christ, this does not mean that Christians were victorious over the onslaught of Satan. During the early church period, Christians were fiercely persecuted by both the Roman and Jewish authorities. In fact, a big part of Roman entertainment included throwing Christians into the arena to be eaten by lions—certainly not what the world would view as victorious.

> And Saul was consenting unto his death. And at that **time there was a great persecution against the church** which was at Jerusalem; and they were all scattered abroad throughout the regions of Judaea and Samaria, except the apostles.[37]

In spite of this persecution, Christianity grew and prospered. The introduction to Luke also provides an excellent picture of the historical account of the biblical record.

> Forasmuch as many have taken in hand to set forth in order a declaration of those things which are most surely believed among us, Even as they delivered them unto us, which from the beginning were **eyewitnesses**, and ministers of the word; It seemed good to me also, having had **perfect understanding of all things from the very first**, to write unto thee in order, most excellent Theophilus, **That thou mightest know the certainty of those things**, wherein thou hast been instructed.[38]

Dan Brown's theory of the victors writing history simply does not hold water. The early Christians were persecuted and put to death, yet the Bible offers a historically accurate account.

---

[36] 1 Corinthians 15:57.
[37] Acts 8:1.
[38] Luke 1:1-4.

3
Complete Disregard of Faith

Ironically, the present day seems to be a time of "open season" on Christianity, while unconditional acceptance and esteem is encouraged on behalf of every other so-called faith. Dan Brown totally disregards faith and considers the Bible a lie. He scorns those who live by faith while revealing his complete misconception of what constitutes faith. According to Brown's mode of reasoning, spiritual truth does not exist anywhere.

> ...**every** faith in the world is based on fabrication. That is the definition of **faith**—acceptance of that which we imagine to be true, that which we cannot prove. [39]

Brown claims that faith is subject to one's imagination. However, God's word is the basis for true faith. He writes that every faith in the world is based on fabrication and thus defines faith as a *fabrication*. Then he narrows his attack to focus on the New Testament, revealing an undeniable disdain for Christianity.

> ...the New Testament is based on fabrications. [40]

Brown writes that the New Testament is based on fabrications. A fabrication is the deliberate act of deviating from the truth—a deception. That would make the New Testament the worst kind of a lie—one that has deceived millions.

---

[39] Brown, p. 341.
[40] Ibid.

The Bible simply defines faith as believing in something without evidence to prove it. For instance, there is no evidence that Jesus shed His own blood for our sin other than the Bible's proclamation of this fact. Therefore, only through faith can an individual believe it to be true.

> Now faith is the substance of things hoped for, the evidence of things not seen.[41]

When someone believes something by faith, he simply believes it without evidence. When an individual believes spiritual things by faith this does not of necessity mean that the object of his faith is untruth. Faith remains an absolute imperative for the Christian to live a life pleasing to the Lord. Contrary to Brown's claims, it is a sin for a Christian to lack the faith that Brown ridicules.

> And he that doubteth is damned if he eat, because he eateth not of faith: **for whatsoever is not of faith is sin.**[42]

> **But without faith it is impossible to please him:** for he that cometh to God must believe that he is, and that he is a rewarder of them that diligently seek him.[43]

The book of Hebrews states that a person without faith cannot please God. Brown further illustrates his ignorance of spiritual matters by claiming that the stories of the Bible are metaphorical and allegorical. Brown claims that these fictional "allegorical stories" have been sold to the world as reality.

---

[41] Hebrews 11:1.
[42] Romans 14:23.
[43] Hebrews 11:6.

> Those who truly understand their faiths understand the stories are metaphorical .... Religious allegory has become a part of the fabric of reality. And living in that reality helps millions of people cope and be better people. [44]

Brown basically claims that millions of Bible believing people live in a dream world that enables them to cope with reality. By carrying Brown's position to its ultimate conclusion, the biblical accounts of Adam and Eve, Abraham, Isaac and Jacob, the Flood, the destruction of the walls of Jericho, etc. are simply allegorical. But the Bible is based on the revelation of God and not simply representations of reality. In fact, the *general* revelation of God refers to that which can be seen by all humankind in His creation.

> **For the invisible things of him from the creation of the world are clearly seen,** being understood by the things that are made, even his eternal power and Godhead; so that they are without excuse:[45]

God's *special* revelation can be found in His word. For instance, the Gospel is a part of God's special revelation. God insured that His chosen men spoke as they were moved by the Holy Ghost. The Son of God also portrays a physical revelation of the Father.

> Jesus saith unto him, Have I been so long time with you, and yet hast thou not known me, Philip? **he that hath seen me hath seen the Father**; and how sayest thou then, Shew us the Father? [46]

---

[44] Brown, p. 342.
[45] Romans 1:20.
[46] John 14:9.

God has revealed Himself to mankind in both a general and special way. By missing His revelation the individual will remain in darkness without light and without hope.

Direct Attack upon Christianity

In each epoch of time, God has always insured that He had a prophet (like Moses) or an apostle (like Matthew, Mark, Paul or Peter) to record history for us. His miraculous works were always accompanied by His word and never left to the private interpretation of others. In contrast, Dan Brown claims that the Gospel has pagan origins.

> Nothing in Christianity is original. The pre-Christian God Mithras—**called the Son of God and the Light of the World**—was born on December 25, died, was buried in a rock tomb, and then resurrected in three days. By the way, December 25 is also the birthday of Osiris, Adonis, and Dionysus. The newborn Krishna was presented with gold, frankincense, and myrrh. Even Christianity's weekly holy day was stolen from the pagans. [47]

We do *not* know the date of Christ's birth, yet this does not mean that the celebration of Christmas or recognition of the birth of Christ is something that must be completely frowned upon. All Christian beliefs and symbols are not totally independent of outside influences. However, the symbols incorporated into worship are never to distract from our worship of Jesus Christ. Regretfully, they frequently do. The ceremonies, paintings, religious icons, symbolism and rituals that drew from pagan practices have no place in the worship of Christ. Frequently these items do distract attention from their object and block one's focus from the truth. *The Da Vinci Code* hones in on some of this symbolism within certain

---

[47] Brown, p. 232.

organizations and reveals its potential danger.

Even if the Christmas calendar date was originally pagan in nature, celebrating it in remembrance of Christ is a good alternative to the pagan festival. We can choose to remember the Lord's birth on this date and draw people's attention to Him by having family gatherings and observing a time when almost all secular work grinds to a halt. Regardless of the dates, origins and absolute accuracy of this date, we do know that it was God the Son who split time into BC and AD by His physical birth into our world. This fact holds true even if our calendars do not reflect the precise year.

In paganism and Greek mythology, the pagan gods usually are said to have come down and had sex with human women, giving birth to super humans or a part human, part god mixture. This is not what happened with the birth of Christ when the Holy Spirit impregnated Mary. She was merely providing a human body in which the Son of God would dwell and eventually die for the sins of mankind.

> The vestiges of pagan religion in Christian symbology are undeniable. Egyptian sun disks became the halos of Catholic saints. Pictograms of Isis nursing her miraculously conceived son Horus became the blueprint for our modern images of the Virgin Mary nursing Baby Jesus. And virtually all the elements of the Catholic ritual—the miter, the altar, the doxology, and communion, the act of "God-eating"—were taken directly from earlier pagan mystery religions.[48]

It is a fact that the halos of the so-called saints have pagan origins and are simply unnecessary artistic depictions composed by sinful men. Assuredly, many of these artists meant well. The pictures of Mary nursing Jesus are simply out of

---

[48] Ibid.

line. Many of the rituals also are extra-biblical so their origins are irrelevant and their incorporation into "worship" is scripturally unwarranted. Yet, many of the other possible pagan similarities don't always predate Christ. In fact, pagans were frequently known to steal from Christianity.

Many times these pagan similarities come not from the actual event that took place, but from the prophecy that preceded the event by hundreds of years or more. For example, Isaiah prophesied of Christ's miraculous birth 750 years prior to His incarnation. These pagan religions appropriated their versions of a virgin birth by stealing from that prophecy.

> Therefore the Lord himself shall give you a sign; Behold, **a virgin shall conceive**, and bear a son, and shall call his name Immanuel.[49]

The virgin birth is not the only parallel story hijacked by paganism. Satan and his pagan cohorts knew of the coming Messiah and would go to any lengths to draw people's attention away from the truth.

After Christ's birth and death, the cults became even more desperate, inventing their own versions of the miraculous. They imitated God's miracles and produced their own pagan substitutes.

Most of the divine man accounts from the mystery religions postdate Christianity. The supposed scholars certainly can't say that Christianity copied paganism. So they change their tactics by pointing out that Christ is not alone in the claims made about Himself. According to these would-be scholars, the Christian faith is therefore not unique, but is some type of imitation faith with pagan origins.

---

[49] Isaiah 7:14.

The Bible

Dan Brown decided for everyone that God could not be trusted to keep His word. He says that the Bible is simply a product of man. This is his opinion and must be refuted. This is what the Bible says:

> For the prophecy came not in old time by the will of man: but holy men of God spake as they were moved by the Holy Ghost.[50]

The Bible is inspired by God or God-breathed. God used individuals to compose and record it without error.

> **All scripture is** given by inspiration of God, and is **profitable** for doctrine, for reproof, for correction, for instruction in righteousness:[51]

What does Dan Brown say? Basically, he says that the Bible is unprofitable and that it originated with man rather than God.

> The Bible is a product of **man**,... Not of God. The Bible did not fall magically from the clouds. Man created it as a historical record of tumultuous times, and it has evolved through countless translations, additions, and revisions. History has never had a definitive version of the book.[52]

Brown's writings reveal his lack of theological credentials. Each individual involved in the writing of scripture submitted his personal will to the Lord. God supernaturally intervened so

---

[50] 2 Peter 1:21.
[51] 2 Timothy 3:16.
[52] Brown, p. 231.

that these men would not err. This act still involves the freewill along with supernatural intervention. Paul commended the Thessalonians for accepting his epistles as the word of God. We too can have the same commendation if we will accept God's word as God's truth, rather than trying to attribute it to man.

> For this cause also thank we God without ceasing, because, when ye received **the word of God** which ye heard of us, ye received it **not as the word of men,** but **as it is in truth, the word of God**, which effectually worketh also in you that believe.[53]

The Bible is not simply the opinion of the writer. Furthermore, most scripture is based on eyewitness testimony.

> For we have not followed cunningly devised fables, when we made known unto you the power and coming of our Lord Jesus Christ, but were **eyewitnesses of his majesty.** [54]

The Holy Spirit Who controlled the writings of the individual books, certainly controlled their selection and collection into the canon of scripture as well. If God gave man His word, He certainly did not leave the choice of which writings were His word up to man. Not so according to Dan Brown:

> More than **eighty** gospels were considered for the New Testament, and yet only a relative few were chosen for inclusion—Matthew, Mark, Luke, and John among them.
>
> Who chose which gospels to include?" Sophie asked.

---

[53] 1 Thessalonians 2:13.
[54] 2 Peter 1:16.

"Aha!" Teabing burst in with enthusiasm. "The fundamental irony of Christianity! The Bible, as we know it today, was collated by the pagan Roman emperor Constantine the Great." [55]

The supposed "eighty gospels" are a figment of Brown's sheer fantasy. History reveals that there were only twelve other gospels in circulation during this period and that none of these other writings was accepted by the churches as inspired. These other works had no "chain of evidence" which connected them with the apostles, and they contained contradictory information from that embodied within the canonical Gospels. Their breadth of distribution and proportion of acceptance were also severely limited.

Christian leaders (called the church fathers) all quoted from the four Gospels. Many of them stated that they considered these books to contain the actual words of Jesus. In fact, almost the entire four Gospels can be recreated in their entirety from a collation of the early writers' quotations. Modern historians and other fictional writers like Dan Brown have gotten things backwards. The early historians would have far more credibility than some fictional author attempting to spin a tale.

Eusebius of Caesarea (275-339AD) was a contemporary of Constantine (A.D. 272-337). He wrote *The History of the Church: from Christ to Constantine*. Although he was a great admirer of Constantine, he never mentioned him as having any role in collating or determining the canon of scripture (that is, the books of the Bible). [56]

The New Testament books did not become authoritative because they were formally included in a canonical list. On

---

[55] Brown, p. 231.

[56] Eusebius, *The History of the Church from Christ to Constantine*, translated by G.S. Williamson, (Harmondsworth, Middlesex, England: Penguin Books, 1983).

the contrary, they were included in the list because they were already considered divinely inspired. The two councils (Hippo Regius in 393 and the one in Carthage in 397) simply codified that which was established practice. They did not impose something new and alien on the church.

Biblical scholar Robert Grant, in *The Formation of the New Testament*, writes that the New Testament canon was:

> ...not the product of official assemblies or even of the studies of a few theologians. It reflects and expresses the ideal self-understanding of a whole religious movement which, in spite of temporal, geographical, and even ideological differences, could finally be united in accepting these 27 diverse documents as expressing the meaning of God's revelation in Jesus Christ and to his church. [57]

It is completely inaccurate to credit our modern day Bible to a man. God supernaturally led the true believers to accept the true writings and reject the spurious ones. Brown considers God impotent and devises some Constantine conspiracy theory speculation.

> "Constantine commissioned and financed a new Bible, which omitted those gospels that spoke of Christ's **human** traits and embellished those gospels that made Him godlike. The earlier gospels were outlawed, gathered up, and burned. ...the modern Bible was compiled and edited by men who possessed a political agenda—to promote the divinity of the man Jesus Christ and use His influence to solidify their own power base." [58]

---

[57] Robert M. Grant, *The Formation of the New Testament* (Harper and Row, 1965), 10.
[58] Brown, p. 234.

...the early Church needed to convince the world that the mortal prophet Jesus was a **divine** being. Therefore, any gospels that described **earthly** aspects of Jesus' life had to be omitted from the Bible. [59]

These three statements would mean that Christ and Christianity are completely false. But Constantine had nothing to do with determining the canon of scripture. If Constantine or some council determined what constituted scripture in the fourth century, what did the people use prior to this time?

Even the Bible gives us examples of early acceptance of scripture. For example, the Apostle Paul joined an Old Testament reference and a New Testament reference in 1 Timothy 5:18 and called them both (collectively) "scripture."

> For the scripture saith, Thou shalt not muzzle the ox that treadeth out the corn. And, The labourer is worthy of his reward.[60]

> **Thou shalt not muzzle the ox when he treadeth out the corn.**[61]

> And in the same house remain, eating and drinking such things as they give: for **the labourer is worthy of his hire**. Go not from house to house.[62]

In his letter to Timothy, Paul recognized the books of Deuteronomy and Luke as canonical. This occurred three centuries before Constantine arrived on the scene.

---

[59] Ibid, p. 244.
[60] 1 Timothy 5:18.
[61] Deuteronomy 25:4.
[62] Luke 10:7.

Paul's recognition of the Old Testament passage as "scripture" was certainly not unusual. However, his reference to a New Testament book as "scripture" so soon after it was written points to the fact that these volumes were immediately considered authoritative by the apostles themselves. Only a few years had elapsed between the writing of Luke's Gospel (A.D. 63) and the writing of First Timothy (A.D. 65). Yet, Paul does not hesitate to place Luke on the same level of authority as the Old Testament book of Deuteronomy.

Paul's reference further proves that man certainly did not have to wait until the fourth century to find out which books constituted the canon of scripture. The Holy Spirit was busy revealing these truths to the apostles and Christians as a whole. The Holy Spirit was busy revealing these truths to the world at large. Paul also recognized his own writings as inspired scripture.

> If any man think himself to be a prophet, or spiritual, **let him acknowledge that the things that I write unto you are the commandments of the Lord.** [63]

The Apostle Paul knew that he was writing inspired scripture, as did many of those that received his letters. The canon of scripture was determined long before the council of Laodicea in AD 363. This council simply confirmed that which the God-honoring Christians had already confirmed through usage long before any council decreed anything. To claim otherwise makes the will of God subservient to the council and not the other way around.

Dan Brown also claims that the lost manuscripts correct that which the churches have used for almost two thousand years. He says:

---

[63] 1 Corinthians 14:37.

"...the Nag Hammadi and Dead Sea Scrolls... [are] "The earliest Christian records." [64]

The Nag Hammadi Texts are named as such because they were found on the west bank of the Nile. Dan Brown claims that they were *scrolls*, but they were actually *codices*, early forms of a book. These writings were rejected by the early Christians because of their uninspired, non-apostolic nature. The Bible reveals that the oldest does not mean the best since there were **many** people who were trying to corrupt the word of God from the very beginning. Paul wrote:

> For we are not as many, which corrupt the word of God: but as of sincerity, but as of God, in the sight of God speak we in Christ.[65]

If Paul wrote of many who were corrupting the word of God in the first century, is it wise to allow the antiquity of a text to determine its authenticity and canonicity? The *Jesus Seminar* is using the Gnostic Gospels in an attempt to redefine the contents of the canon of scripture. Brown is falling for the same rewriting of church history by reinterpreting the Christian faith using Gnostic "spirituality."

Whom do we trust—God or some pagan ruler? In 312 A.D., Constantine was proclaimed emperor of the West. The following year he proclaimed tolerance of all religions. This would seem like a victory for the faith; however, the truth is the only thing that can withstand persecution and flourishes from it.

Constantine's politicizing of Christianity and the creation of a state-sponsored church was detrimental to true biblical Christianity. Up until Constantine's vision which he interpreted to be Christian, the practice of Christianity had

---

[64] Brown, p. 245.
[65] 2 Corinthians 2:17.

been essentially illegal in the Roman Empire. Christians were tortured and imprisoned for the faith.

Constantine's edict of toleration ended the persecution and made various forms of Christianity preferred. He used this political maneuver to unite the kingdom and strengthen his position. The Christian churches ended up with a redefinition of what it meant to be a Christian—how one becomes a Christian. Rather than experiencing an authentic conversion to Christianity for spiritual reasons, now it was politically expedient to claim to be a Christian. Many of the pagan worshipers willingly embraced Christianity because it was now the acceptable form of worship.

This huge influx of pagans now calling themselves Christians created a lukewarm type of "Christian" service. Rome has continually grown to become an all encompassing religious-political institution. However, the claim that Constantine gave us the Bible and preserved the truth for all future believers is a lie being further perpetrated by Dan Brown's book.

Sunday Worship

Not only does Dan Brown credit Constantine with giving us the Bible, but he also claims that the emperor determined Sunday to be the day set aside for worship.

> "Originally," Langdon said, "Christianity honored the Jewish Sabbath of Saturday, but Constantine shifted it to coincide with the pagan's veneration day of the sun." He paused, grinning. "To this day, most churchgoers attend services on Sunday morning with no idea that they are there on account of the pagan sun god's weekly tribute—*Sunday*." [66]

Christianity honored Sunday—the first day of the week—long before Constantine was even born.

---

[66] Brown, p. 232-233.

Some of the confusion with certain groups arises today when they consider that the Apostle Paul repeatedly went into the synagogue on *the Sabbath Day* to witness to the Jews. However, common sense would dictate that it is best to enter the synagogue on the day when the Jews were worshipping—that is, Saturday—the seventh day of the week.

The central hope and foundation of Christianity—the Resurrection—occurred on *the first day of the week*. The Bible says that the Christians followed this pattern by coming together on that day to celebrate their new life in Christ.

> **Now when Jesus was risen early the first day of the week**, he appeared first to Mary Magdalene, out of whom he had cast seven devils.[67]

> **And upon the first day of the week, when the disciples came together** to break bread, Paul preached unto them, ready to depart on the morrow; and continued his speech until midnight. [68]

> **Upon the first day of the week** let every one of you lay by him in store, as God hath prospered him, that there be no gatherings when I come.[69]

Numerous examples exist showing us that the early church fathers specified Resurrection day as the day that they came together to worship—independent of and prior to the influence of Constantine. Ignatius, Bishop of Antioch (110 AD), specified the "Lord's Day" as the one on which our life arises through Him. This is a clear definitive example that the churches of the first century no longer followed the Jewish Sabbath but congregated on Sunday instead.

---

[67] Mark 16:9.
[68] Acts 20:7.
[69] 1 Corinthians 16:2.

If, then, those who walk in the ancient practices attain to newness of hope, no longer observing the Sabbath, but fashioning their lives after **the Lord's Day on which our life also arose through Him**, that we may be found disciples of Jesus Christ, our only teacher.[70]

Justin Martyr (150 AD) also described Sunday as the day when Christians gathered to read the scriptures and hold their assembly because it is both the initial day of creation and the day of Christ's Resurrection. There were also many other church fathers whose testimonies reveal that the early church followed the New Testament example of coming together on Sunday (the first day of the week), rather than on the Jewish Sabbath. These testimonies all predate Constantine.

---

[70] http://en.wikipedia.org/wiki/Ignatius_of_Antioch

4
Patriarchal vs. Matriarchal Religion

It is no secret that the Bible and Christianity are male dominated. The leadership roles—the pastors and deacons—are filled by men. Christ's apostles were twelve chosen *men*. Paul, Barnabas, Matthias and all of the other apostles after the twelve were likewise men. Brown claims that Judaism and Christianity were both hijacked by the men and these patriarchal systems were originally set up as matriarchal.

Dan Brown would have us believe that Christianity was concocted in order to subjugate women. He writes that Jesus actually chose a woman to be its goddess and never intended Christianity to be patriarchal. Here is Brown's hypothesis:

> Constantine and his male successors successfully converted the world from matriarchal paganism to patriarchal Christianity by waging a campaign of propaganda that demonized the sacred feminine, obliterating the goddess from modern religion forever.[71]

This is pure revisionism with no historical support whatsoever. Constantine did politicize his version of Christianity after seeing "a bright image of a cross in the sky inscribed with the words 'Conquer by this.'" He battled under the sign of the cross and took control of the Roman Empire and the persecution against the followers of Christ ceased. This is the kernel of truth that makes Brown's conspiracy theory plausible.

When limited factual information is interlaced with believable fiction, and fiction is peddled for fact, the conspiracy advocate looking for a boogeyman under every bush is

---

[71] Brown, p. 124.

lured into a quagmire of his own making. Brown's delusional interpretations mean that the whole world has been conned. In fact, Brown writes that:

> ...powerful men in the early Christian church 'conned' the world by propagating lies that devalued the female and tipped the scales in favor of the masculine. [72]

According to this line of thinking, one would expect to discover some evidence of a female dominated Christianity or society during the first centuries after Christ. However, no such evidence exists. Since there is no historical evidence of a matriarchal society, the million dollar question is how could Constantine have converted society to a patriarchal system? There is nothing in the "historical record" to prove that any matriarchal society existed during the first century. In fact, there is no proof that such a society *ever* existed.

Steven Goldberg, chairman of the Department of Sociology at City College of the City University of New York, has devoted his career to exposing the "fallacious reasoning, misrepresenting of fact, and ideological agendas in social sciences."[73] He exposed the non-existence of matriarchal societies in his book *Why Men Rule: A Theory of Male Dominance*.

> Patriarchy is any system of organization (political, economic, industrial, financial, religious, or social) in which the overwhelming number of upper positions in hierarchies are occupied by males. ...The point is that authority and leadership are, and always have been, associated with the male in every society, and I refer to this when I say that patriarchy is universal and that there has never been a matriarchy. [74]

---

[72] Ibid.

[73] His biography on Amazon.com: http://www.amazon.com/gp/product/1591020042/104-8214946-3835941?v=glance&n=283155

[74] Steven Goldberg, *Why Men Rule: A Theory of Male Dominance*, (New York, NY: Open Court Publishing Co., 1994) p. 14.

Likewise, theories that hypothesized a matriarchal form of society at 'an earlier stage in history' made a certain, if tortuous, sense until the findings of the past 50 years failed to include a single shred of evidence that such matriarchies had ever existed, and demonstrated the inability of all such theories to deal with reality. [75]

If a male led society is virtually universal, where does Dan Brown's theory originate? In the same book, Goldberg quotes noted anthropologist Margaret Mead[76] as agreeing with his position:

> It is true...that all the claims so glibly made about societies ruled by women are nonsense. We have no reason to believe that they ever existed. ...men everywhere have been in charge of running the show. ...men have been the leaders in public affairs and the final authorities at home. (Quoted from *Redbook*, October 1973, p. 48). [77]

With the debunking of Brown's "historical record" fantasy concerning the supposed dismantling of matriarchal societies, it is important to understand that believing the truth does not make someone a male chauvinist. The emphasis on a patriarchal system does not degrade or belittle women. The feminists would have the world believe that Christians are a

---

[75] Ibid., p. 18.
[76] Margaret Mead received a Ph.D. from Columbia University where she eventually taught as an adjunct professor. She was considered by some of her colleagues as the most renowned anthropologist of all time. She produced 44 books and more than 1,000 articles. She was also a strong proponent of women's rights which makes her assessment all the more unbiased.
http://www.cas.usf.edu/anthropology/women/mead/margaret_mead.htm
[77] Goldberg, p. 35.

bunch of male elitists offering no place for women to serve the Saviour. Brown writes for this type audience and those duped into swallowing their line of reasoning.

Brown has his Langdon character depict Christianity as being anti-woman and repressive. Brown obviously knows nothing of what we would term *biblical* Christianity, in contrast to systems of religion that simply call themselves Christian. The Bible and true Christianity do not repress women. Husbands are to love their wives and give themselves for their wives. There is no greater security for a woman than to be truly loved in that capacity and with such magnitude.

> **Husbands, love your wives**, even as Christ also loved the church, and gave himself for it; [78]

Unlike some non-Christian pagan societies, Christianity does not teach that women are without rights and are the property of their husbands. Consider how women are treated in predominantly Muslim countries. In many cases Muslim women are not allowed to be educated, or to show their faces in public or even speak publicly. Sex-selection infanticide is still common today in China where female babies are aborted. Some pagan tribes even expect the wife to follow her husband in death. Are we to believe that these societies are superior to a truly Bible-based Christian society just because some inequities can be found within these societies?

The Bible offers a picture of women far removed from the repressed state claimed by Brown. Men were to be women's protectors. The Bible portrays women as the weaker vessels—which is not meant to be condescending toward women in any way. When realistic facts are presented, they should be accepted as such.

---

[78] Ephesians 5:25.

> Likewise, ye husbands, dwell with them according to knowledge, **giving honour unto the wife, as unto the weaker vessel**, and as being heirs together of the grace of life; that your prayers be not hindered. [79]

Male chauvinism has a bad connotation, but some present day chivalry would certainly be refreshing. The Bible extols the virtues of many famous and courageous women—Esther, Ruth, Debra, as well as the virtuous woman of Proverbs chapter 31. This is certainly a picture far removed from the repressed womanhood claimed by Brown.

It was a woman to whom Jesus first announced the fact that He was the Messiah.[80] It was the women that first testified regarding the Resurrection of Christ.[81] The story of Mary and Martha is another prime example of the importance of getting the story straight. Mary chose to sit at the feet of Jesus while Martha fulfilled the role of hostess. Jesus commended Mary's actions, while challenging Martha's preoccupation with physical labor.

> Now it came to pass, as they went, that he entered into a certain village: and a certain woman named Martha received him into her house. And she had a sister called Mary, which also sat at Jesus' feet, and heard his word. **But Martha was cumbered about much serving**, and came to him, and said, Lord, dost thou not care that my sister hath left me to serve alone? bid her therefore that she help me. And Jesus answered and said unto her, Martha, Martha, thou art careful and troubled about many things: **But one thing is needful: and Mary hath chosen that good part, which shall not be taken away from her.** [82]

---

[79] 1 Peter 3:7.
[80] See Luke 10:25-26.
[81] See Matthew 28:7.
[82] Luke 10:38-42.

Dan Brown would have us believe that a matriarchal pagan female deity culture that never existed is superior to a Judeo-Christian culture. The Bible elevates women and specifically defines their roles. It is the Gnostic documents that denigrate women, portraying them as defective beings.

For example, saying 114 of *The Gospel of Thomas* quotes Simon Peter as saying to Jesus, *"Let Mary leave us, for women are not worthy of life." Jesus responded, "I myself shall lead her in order to make her male, so that she too may become a living spirit resembling you males. For every woman who will make herself male will enter the Kingdom of Heaven."* [83]

Many cultish groups are heading toward a female dominated paganism as prescribed by the father of lies—Satan himself. Dan Brown is simply rewriting history, further influencing the fringe groups toward his type of religious expression. Those who are not completely Bible based, but claim to be followers of Christ, will fall for the deception.

Dan Brown's book points to the Bible and Christianity as being deficient. Yet, the materials he claims superior are in fact guilty of propagating the very thing he condemns. Gnostic "Christians" sought to transform Christianity into one of the pagan mystery religions that were flourishing in the ancient world. The Gnostics were the persecutors of women while the Christians truly placed them on a pedestal. *The Da Vinci Code*:

> "Fortunately for historians... some of the gospels that Constantine attempted to eradicate managed to survive. **The Dead Sea Scrolls were found in the 1950s**[84] hidden

---

[83] Section 114

[84] Another of the blunders by Dan Brown's "expert"—the Dead Sea Scrolls were discovered in *1947*, not in the 1950s. They did not contain anything mentioning Jesus at all. In fact, most of the scrolls predate the New Testament and do not contain Christian texts at all. They came from a monastic Jewish sect known as the Essenes. Jesus, Mary Magdalene and the Grail are not even mentioned in them.

in a cave near Qumran in the Judean desert. And, of course, the Coptic Scrolls in 1945 at Nag Hammadi. In addition to telling **the true Grail story**, these documents speak of Christ's ministry in very human terms.... The scrolls highlight glaring historical discrepancies and fabrications, clearly confirming that **the modern Bible was compiled and edited by men who possessed a political agenda— to promote the divinity of the man Jesus Christ** and use His influence to solidify their own power base." [85]

The Gnostic Gospels touted as the true word of God by Dan Brown are generally dated to the second and third centuries. Therefore, the writers were not apostles or even direct disciples of the Lord, nor were they eyewitnesses of Jesus' life. There has always been a deviant strand of "Christianity" that wrote its own scripture. These sources are certainly not more trustworthy than the time-tested, authoritative Bible we hold in our hands.

The evidentiary matter supporting the text of the Bible includes manuscript evidence, internal linguistic evidence and external attestation to the veracity of the material. The patriarchal makeup of the Jewish culture externally attests to the veracity of the paternalistic design of the church, while the matriarchal Gnostic Gospels have no external attestation in history. Irenaeus wrote of the spurious writings existing during the second century.

Irenaeus (A.D. 130-200) wrote in his work *Adversus Haereses* (*Against Heresies*) about, *"an unspeakable number of apocryphal and spurious writings, which they themselves* [referring to heretics] *had forged, to bewilder the minds of the foolish."* [86]

The warnings are both historical and scriptural. As we

---

[85] Brown, p. 234.
[86] Irenaeus, ADVERSUS HAERESES, i.20.1.

have already seen, Paul referred to the same problem cited by Irenaeus. There were many people corrupting the word of God even as the true scripture was being penned.

> For we are not as many, which corrupt the word of God: but as of sincerity, but as of God, in the sight of God speak we in Christ.[87]

One of the Gnostic Gospels discovered at Nag Hammadi in 1945 is *The Gospel of Truth*, about which Irenaeus says: *"It agrees in nothing with the Gospels of the Apostles, so that they have really no Gospel which is not full of blasphemy. For if what they have published is the Gospel of Truth, and yet is totally unlike those which have been handed down to us by the Apostles,...* [then] *that which has been handed down from the Apostles can no longer be reckoned the Gospel of Truth."*

In other words, the Gnostic Gospels contradict the canonical Gospels which have proven to be true. Therefore, you must accept one or the other, but certainly not both.

The *Gospel of Thomas* was discovered in Nag Hammadi, Egypt, near Cairo in 1945 and was translated into English in 1977. While some "scholars" have attempted to date parts of it earlier, the *Gospel of Thomas* is most reliably dated no earlier than A.D. 140-170. This spurious writing contains 114 supposed secret sayings of Jesus. It portrays a second century Gnosticism which was prevalent at that time. This work parallels many New Age teachings today.[88]

The *Gospel of Thomas* begins with these words: *"These are the **secret sayings** which the living Jesus spoke..."* However, notice the true record of what Jesus said about those that would one day claim He spoke in secret.

---

[87] 2 Corinthians 2:17.

[88] THE NAG HAMMADI LIBRARY, ed. James M. Robinson (San Francisco: Harper & Row Publishers, 1978), p. 118.

Jesus answered him, I spake openly to the world; I ever taught in the synagogue, and in the temple, whither the Jews always resort; and **in secret have I said nothing.** [89]

The Lord's omniscience allowed Him to peremptorily dispel heretical claims. Here is another example of what we are being told is now the truth: *"Every woman who will make herself male will enter the Kingdom of Heaven."* [90]

Did man really have to wait four centuries, or worse yet twenty centuries for some Egyptian manuscripts to be discovered, to know the truth? The New Testament itself reveals that a collection of books existed in the first century. Peter speaks of having Paul's epistles and considering them to be on par with Old Testament scripture.

> And account that the longsuffering of our Lord is salvation; even as our beloved brother **Paul** also according to the wisdom given unto him hath **written unto you**; As also in **all his epistles**, speaking in them of these things; in which are some things hard to be understood, which they that are unlearned and unstable wrest, as they do also the other scriptures, unto their own destruction.[91]

Peter recognized Paul's writings as inspired, just as Paul recognized Luke's to be inspired by God in 1 Timothy 5:18. The Bible tells us that the churches were instructed to send their epistle to other churches as well.

> And when **this epistle** is read among you, cause that it **be read also in the church of the Laodiceans**; and that ye likewise read the epistle from Laodicea.[92]

---

[89] John 18:20.
[90] Gregory Boyd, *Jesus Under Siege* (Wheaton, IL: Victor, 1995), p. 118.
[91] 2 Peter 3:15-16.
[92] Colossians 4:16.

The New Testament is verified by many lines of evidence, including self-references, early canonical lists, thousands of citations by the early church fathers and the well-established dates for the Synoptic Gospels. The same cannot be said concerning the Gnostic Gospels. The teachings of the Gnostic Gospels were anti-scriptural and sometimes heretical.

Among other things, the Gnostics taught that:

1. The supreme achievement of human life is the attainment of a direct, personal and absolute knowledge of the authentic truths of existence (of course, apart from the Bible—allegedly through someone like James or Mary Magdalene).

2. There exists both a transcendent God and a lower God (the Creator-Demiurge), whom Gnostics equated with Yahweh of the Old Testament.

3. To know oneself is to know God and the secret of gnosis. Self-knowledge is the knowledge of God.

4. Spirit is good and matter is evil.

5. Man's spirit is imprisoned in the material body but will escape its imprisonment at death.

6. There is no physical resurrection of the body. [93]

According to Gnostic teaching, ignorance—rather than sin—is man's primary problem.[94] According to Dan Brown:

---

[93] TEACHINGS OF SILVANUS, 85.24-106.14, in NAG HAMMADI LIBRARY, pp. 347-56; cited by Pagels, GNOSTIC GOSPELS (New York: Random House, 1979), p. 127.
And http://www.webcom.com/gnosis/naghamm/nhlintro.html
[94] THE BIBLICAL WORLD, ed. Charles F. Pfeiffer (Grand Rapids: Baker Book House, 1976), p. 405.

"Early Jews believed that the Holy of Holies in Solomon's Temple housed not only God but also His powerful female equal, Shekinah." [95]

The early Jews believed nothing of the sort—this is simple revisionism. The Bible teaches of one God—monotheism, not some sort of plurality of gods and there is no record of a female counterpart to the male God.

Hear, O Israel: **The LORD our God is one LORD**: [96]

The Old Testament Hebrew references to *shekinah* refer to *the glory of God*, not some "powerful female equal" as the Gnostics claim.

The "Shekinah" refers to the glory of God,[97] not to some *"powerful female equal."* "Shekinah" comes from a Hebrew word literally meaning "to inhabit." God would appear in the cloud above the mercy seat within the Tabernacle. Dan Brown uses his authoritative speaking characters (for example, a Harvard professor) to create the elusion of credibility. For example:

"The Jewish tetragrammaton YHWH—the sacred name of God—in fact derived from Jehovah, an androgynous physical union between the masculine Jah and the pre-Hebraic name for Eve, Havah." [98]

Now that sounds real good and very educated! Dan Brown says that the sacred tetragrammaton YHWH came

---

[95] Brown, p. 309.
[96] Deuteronomy 6:4
[97] Exodus 25:22; Leviticus 16:2; Ezekiel 9:3; 10:18; Hebrews 9:5.
[98] Brown, p. 309.

from Jehovah. The term "YHWH" was not derived from "Jehovah"; rather, "Jehovah" was derived from "YHWH." Brown got it backwards! The Old Testament contains the name YHWH because the original Hebrew had only consonants. It is believed that the scribes formed a new word (Jehovah) by inserting the vowels from Adonai (a-o- a) into the consonants, YHWH. The result was Yahowah, or Jehovah. This is just one more of the many inaccuracies contained in this supposedly historical book.

5
Messiah or Mere Mortal

The belief in the Deity of Christ is one of the fundamentals of the faith. Christ's Deity means that He is God and not simply human. Brown claims that Christ's divinity (or Deity) was a fourth century invention. Satan has always vehemently attacked the Deity of Christ, knowing that Christ's Deity singularly qualifies Him to be our Saviour. Dan Brown's subtle and sometimes overt attack is veiled in a fictional book which he claims to be historically factual.

> "Indeed," Teabing said. "...During this fusion of religions, Constantine needed to strengthen the new Christian tradition, and held a famous ecumenical gathering known as the Council of Nicaea."... "At this gathering...many aspects of Christianity were debated and voted upon—the date of Easter, the role of the bishops. The administration of sacraments, and of course, the **divinity** of Jesus."
>
> [Sophie] "I don't follow. His divinity?"
>
> "My dear," Teabing declared, "**until that moment in history, Jesus was viewed by His followers as a mortal prophet...** a great and powerful man, but a **man** nonetheless. A mortal."
>
> [Sophie] "Not the Son of God?"
>
> "Right," Teabing said. "Jesus' establishment as 'the Son of God' was officially proposed and voted on by the Council of Nicaea."
>
> [Sophie] "Hold on. You're saying Jesus' divinity was the result of a vote?"
>
> "A relatively close vote at that," Teabing added...**Constantine turned Jesus into a deity...**" [99]

---

[99] Brown, p. 233.

This is sheer blasphemy!

Constantine and the Council did *not* establish anything. In this case, the Council merely *affirmed* that which the Bible and Christians had been teaching about Jesus' divinity since 33AD and that which the word of God had already prophesied. To claim otherwise is to ignore the facts of history and the truth of scripture. Dan Brown's rhetoric sounds like music to the ears of groups like the Jehovah's Witnesses who also reject Christ's Deity. Brown's blasphemous attack continues:

> "Many scholars claim that the early Church literally stole Jesus from His original followers, **hijacking His human message, shrouding it in an impenetrable cloak of divinity**, and using it to expand their own power." [100]

These statements make the *Da Vinci Code* a sheer work of fiction and a blasphemous one at that. The New Testament writers themselves recognized that Jesus was absolute Deity. Many verses prove that His divinity was not something fabricated by those attempting to expand their power base. Jesus' own words show His equality with the Father.

I and my Father are one.[101]

Jesus was either God manifest in the flesh or a liar. The fact is that Jesus is the Creator of Genesis chapter 1. When you read in the first chapter of Genesis the words *"And God said..."* in verses 3, 6, 9, 11, 14, 20, 24, 26, 28 and 29, you are reading what God the Son said. The Bible says that everything was created by Him and for Him and ***for His pleasure.***

---

[100] Ibid.
[101] John 10:30

Thou art worthy, O Lord, to receive glory and honour and power: **for thou hast created all things, and for thy pleasure they are and were created.** [102]

God the Father created all things through the Son.

For by him [the Son] **were all things created,** that are in heaven, and that are in earth, visible and invisible, whether they be thrones, or dominions, or principalities, or powers: all things were created by him, and for him: [103]

Because He is the Creator and Saviour, Christians are to be looking for Jesus Christ to return and catch us up together to be with Him forever. Christians are looking for THE great God (Jesus Christ) and OUR Saviour (Jesus Christ through a personal relationship). It takes a personal relationship to make Jesus one's Saviour, but no such decision must be made for Him to be THE great God. Only Christians can claim to be...

Looking for that blessed hope, and the glorious appearing of **the great God and our Saviour Jesus Christ;** [104]

Brown claims that the 300 bishops convened the Council of Nicea basically believing that Jesus was a mortal prophet until Constantine told them to turn Him into deity. The witnesses of the New Testament along with the first 300 years of Christian thinking and worship prove that the churches prior to Constantine believed that Christ was God manifest in the flesh.

Here are the facts concerning Constantine: The Council

---

[102] Revelation 4:11.
[103] Colossians 1:16.
[104] Titus 2:13.

convened in A.D. 325 to settle a dispute regarding the nature of Christ caused by the teachings of Arius. The Council was correcting a distortion, certainly not inventing the divinity of Jesus. They were not even deliberating his divinity, but rather whether He was co-eternal with the Father or simply a created being.

Dan Brown's assertion that Jesus was *not* recognized as God until the Council of Nicea[105] voted him as God by a "close vote" is completely untrue. The council of Nicea—which began a blueprint for the Nicean Creed—affirmed Christ's divinity. It simply affirmed the teaching of the churches over the previous three centuries.

As for a vote, the bishops did need to decide whether or not to sign the statement the Council drafted, clarifying their understanding of the historical and biblical teaching concerning Jesus' nature. If this is what Brown meant by a "vote," then it wasn't very close at all: "Only **two** out of more than 300 bishops **failed to sign** the creed!" A 99% vote certainly would not be classified as close. [106]

The two dissenting bishops that were associated with Arius were Secundu of Ptolemais and Theonas of Marmarica. Both of them with Arius went into exile after the council of Nicea. [107]

The Bible also attests to Christ's nature. Jesus claimed this fact and the apostles proclaimed it. Here are just a few of the significant passages which document the Deity of Christ:

> In the beginning was the Word, and the Word was with God, and the Word was God. [108]

---

[105] Convened in A.D. 325 in Asia Minor, present day Turkey.
[106] http://www.reachouttrust.org/articles/relatedsubjects/davinci.htm, (emphasis added).
[107] Timothy D. Barnes, *Constantine and Eusebius*, (Harvard: Presidents and Fellows of Harvard College, 1981).
[108] John 1:1.

And without controversy great is the mystery of godliness: God was manifest in the flesh, justified in the Spirit, seen of angels, preached unto the Gentiles, believed on in the world, received up into glory.[109]

Therefore the Jews sought the more to kill him, because he not only had broken the sabbath, but said also that God was his Father, making himself equal with God. [110] And Thomas answered and said unto him, My Lord and my God.[111]

Looking for that blessed hope, and the glorious appearing of the great God and our Saviour Jesus Christ;[112]

Those at the Council meeting overwhelmingly signed and agreed to the creed because the Deity of Christ was the true teaching of the churches for almost three centuries prior to this time. They simply affirmed that Christ had no beginning.

---

[109] 1 Timothy 3:16.
[110] John 5:18.
[111] John 20:28.
[112] Titus 2:13.

6
Marriage of Jesus and Mary Magdalene

Dan Brown repeatedly refers to statements as being a "matter of the historical record." Of course, there are writers of history on both sides of any issue—each trying to persuade the other side of the legitimacy of their position. The lies of history are just as much a part of the *historical record* as is the truth; however, many times Brown's assertion that something is a part of the historical record is simply artistic license by the author. For example:

> "**It's a matter of the historical record**...and Da Vinci was certainly aware of that fact...**The Last Supper** practically shouts at the viewer that Jesus and Magdalene were a pair." [113]

Dan Brown claims that *The Last* Supper by Leonardo[114] emphatically communicates the news that Jesus and Mary

---

[113] Brown, p. 244.

[114] Another black eye on Dan Brown's scholarship has to do with the way in which he refers to Leonardo da Vinci throughout the book. He repeatedly refers to him as Da Vinci. One glaring example of the shoddy scholarship is found on page 45 where his historical expert refers to Leonardo as "Da Vinci" seven times. He does this here, as well as throughout the entire book. Interestingly, Leonardo da Vinci's name was not *da Vinci* but rather Leonardo. He was born as the illegitimate son of Piero da Vinci in 1452 in the town of Vinci. "Da Vinci" simply means "of Vinci," much like Jesus *of Nazareth* means that He was from Nazareth. It is just as unscholarly to consider "da Vinci" to be Leonardo's last name as it is to consider "of Nazareth" to be the last name of Jesus.

Magdalene were married. He also claims that Peter disapproved of their marriage. According to Brown, the outline of the two figures in the painting (John and Jesus or Mary and Jesus) form the outline of an "M" which indicates that John is really Mary. He says that it is also significant that there was "no chalice" on the table meaning that Mary Magdalene represents the true chalice.

Interpreting *The Last Supper*

Brown misses the point once again. Leonardo's painting does not portray the moment at which Christ instituted the Lord's Supper; thus, the cup is not yet on the table. Rather this painting portrays the moment after Christ has announced that someone at the table would soon betray Him.[115] Notice that the Lord makes this announcement as they were eating.[116]

> **And as they sat and did eat**, Jesus said, Verily I say unto you, One of you which eateth with me shall betray me. [117]
>
> And **as they did eat,** he said, Verily I say unto you, that one of you shall betray me.[118]

The painting shows the twelve apostles' reaction to this announcement as they recoil in horror. In the painting, John, who previously had his head upon Jesus' chest [119] now seems to have Peter whispering into his ear to ask the Lord who it would be that would betray Him.[120] The so-called

---

[115] See Mark 14:18.
[116] See Matthew 26:21.
[117] Mark 14:18.
[118] Matthew 26:21.
[119] See John 13:23.
[120] See John 13:24.

"disembodied hand" could be Peter's hand on John's shoulder as he whispers into his ear.

> Now there was leaning on Jesus' bosom one of his disciples, whom Jesus loved. **Simon Peter** therefore beckoned to him, that he should ask who it should be of whom he spake. [121]

Another of the apostles with his finger in the air looks to be asking, "Is it I?" [122]

> And they began to be sorrowful, and to say unto him one by one, Is it I? and another said, Is it I? [123]

After the apostles each ask in turn who will betray their Lord, Jesus asks that the cup and the bread be placed on the table. John places his head back down where it was and whispers the question to the Lord.[124]

> He then lying on Jesus' breast saith unto him, Lord, who is it? [125]

The other apostles hear the answer,[126] but assume that he is referring to something concerning Judas's position as treasurer.[127]

> Jesus answered, He it is, to whom I shall give a sop, when I have dipped it. And when he had dipped the sop, he gave

---

[121] John 13:23-24.
[122] See Mark 14:19.
[123] Mark 14:19.
[124] See John 13:25.
[125] John 13:25.
[126] See John 13:26-27.
[127] See John 13:28-29.

it to Judas Iscariot, the son of Simon. And after the sop Satan entered into him. Then said Jesus unto him, That thou doest, do quickly. **Now no man at the table knew for what intent he spake this unto him**. For some of them thought, because Judas had the bag, that Jesus had said unto him, Buy those things that we have need of against the feast; or, that he should give something to the poor. He then having received the sop went immediately out: and it was night. [128]

Because John is closest to the Lord when he asks the identity of the betrayer, he was the only one that knew that the Lord was pointing out Judas Iscariot as the betrayer. However, it seems that John also had a difficult time understanding the meaning of Christ's words.

Brown's Circular Reasoning

Dan Brown uses "the historical record" argument once again in the next quote, as though this adds credibility to the position simply by showing that someone claimed something to be a historical fact and wrote about it. Of course, the historical record many times contains things that are mere fabrications.

> "...the marriage of Jesus and Mary Magdalene is **part of the historical record**. ...Moreover, Jesus as a married man makes infinitely more sense than our standard biblical view of Jesus as a bachelor... Because Jesus was a Jew... **the social decorum during that time virtually forbid a Jewish man to be unmarried.** According to Jewish custom, celibacy was condemned, and the obligation for a Jewish father was to find a suitable wife for his son. If Jesus were not married, at least one of the Bible's gospels would have mentioned it and offered some explanation for His unnatural state of bachelorhood. [129]

---

[128] John 13:26-30.
[129] Brown, p. 245.

If Mary was married to Jesus, why didn't the scriptures state this? There is no evidence of His being married during His earthly ministry. Whenever the Bible mentions Christ's family relationships, it mentions His mother and sisters and brothers, but never a wife.

Jesus was not required to marry by governmental or religious law. Brown claims that it was customary for a man of his age to be married. However, it must be remembered that although Jesus took upon Himself the form of human flesh, He was still supernatural and did not fit into any pattern of humanity. He was counter-cultural. To claim that the sinless Son of God had to be like everyone else is ludicrous.

Jesus was not even a rabbi. The Jews asked Jesus "by what authority" He did certain things because He did not hold any kind of formal office within Judaism. He did not have an official Jewish position that would have permitted him to speak with such authority within the temple or even in public. As far as the Jewish leaders were concerned, Jesus had no recognized role within Judaism.

> And say unto him, **By what authority** doest thou these things? and who gave thee this authority to do these things? [130]

Based on the *Gospel of Philip*, Brown asserts in his book that "...the companion of the Saviour is Mary Magdalene. Christ loved her more than all the disciples and used to kiss her often on her mouth. The rest of the disciples were offended by it and expressed disapproval. They said to him, 'Why do you love her more than all of us?'" [131]

Three more glaring errors and contradictions surface

---

[130] Mark 11:28.
[131] Brown, p. 246.

from Brown's points here. First of all, the document in question is missing the key word that people assume is "mouth." There is a hole in the papyrus and the word can only be assumed. The document reads, *"Jesus kissed her often on the..."* To fill it in with "mouth" in the book is dishonest. This papyrus could just as easily read "head" or "cheek."

Secondly, the point about the *Aramaic* scholars is false and misleading too.

> "As any Aramaic scholar will tell you, the word **companion**, in those days, literally meant **spouse**" [132]

The *Gospel of Philip* dates to A.D. 275. This document does not state that Jesus and Mary were married and it was written in *Greek*, not Aramaic as Brown claims. This is quite a blunder for someone trying to convince his readers of the historical veracity of his book.

Even in the Coptic translation found at Nag Hammadi, a Greek loan word (i.e. *koinonos*) lies behind the term translated "companion." Darrell Bock observes that this term *can* mean "wife" or "sister" in a spiritual sense, but it's "not the typical or common term for 'wife'" in Greek.[133]

The third glaring error involves the contradiction about Jesus being married and the disciples' showing their disapproval of the way He treated His supposed wife. If Jesus and Mary Magdalene were in fact married, why would the disciples be offended? Why would they express disapproval if he loved her more than them? You can't have it both ways. John's Gospel mentions the one that Jesus loved—the Apostle John himself—on numerous occasions.[134] Was this terminology really intended to refer to Christ's secret wife instead?

---

[132] Ibid.
[133] Michael Gleghorn, "Decoding the Da Vinci Code," www.probe.org
[134] See John 19:26, 21:27, 20.

Unfortunately, Dan Brown does not stop at simply claiming that Jesus was married. He goes on to say that Jesus and Mary Magdalene also had children together.

> "...the greatest cover-up in human history. Not only was Jesus Christ married, but He was a father. My dear, Mary Magdalene was the Holy Vessel. She was the chalice that bore the royal bloodline of Jesus Christ. She was the womb that bore the lineage, and the vine from which the sacred fruit sprang forth!"[135]

How far fetched can you get? The Bible refers to the children of God on numerous occasions and never indicates that somehow they are His physical descendants. "For ye are all the children of God by faith in Christ Jesus".[136] In fact, the children of God are His descendants through a spiritual rebirth. Becoming a child of God requires faith in Christ Jesus, not some *royal bloodline* through natural means.

Jesus' marriage is yet future. He will one day marry the "bride of Christ." He would be an adulterer if He were already wed to Mary Magdalene.

> Let us be glad and rejoice, and give honour to him: for **the marriage of the Lamb is come, and his wife hath made herself ready**. And to her was granted that she should be arrayed in fine linen, clean and white: for the fine linen is the righteousness of saints. And he saith unto me, Write, Blessed are they which are called unto the marriage supper of the Lamb. And he saith unto me, These are the true sayings of God. [137]

---

[135] Brown, p. 249.
[136] Galatians 3:26.
[137] Revelation 19:7-9.

7

Interpreting the Madonna of the Rocks

The claim that Leonardo intended to communicate anti-Christian secrets through his two versions of the *Madonna of the Rocks*[138] cannot be substantiated. It is true that Leonardo was anti-clerical—against the clergy—because of their well-documented abuses. He criticized the wealth of the clerics and their taking advantage of fearful followers. He criticized the selling of indulgences, and the elaborate honor given to the "saints." But there is no evidence that he had knowledge of some grand conspiracy which he attempted to debunk.

Leonardo received his commission from the **Confraternity of the Immaculate Conception** to paint the picture as the altar centerpiece for the chapel in the church of San Francesco Grande. This group was organized for the purpose of promoting the belief in Mary's Immaculate Conception—the teaching that God preserved Mary from original sin at birth (and then throughout her life). Brown writes:

> The **nuns** gave Leonardo specific dimensions, and the desired theme for the painting...Although Da Vinci did as they requested, when he delivered the work, the group reacted with horror. He had filled the painting with explosive and disturbing details.[139]

Three obvious blunders are readily apparent.

Blunder 1: Brown claims that the "nuns" gave Leonardo

---

[138] One is located at the Louvre; the other is at the National Gallery in London.
[139] Brown, p. 138.

specific dimensions. However, this Confraternity was *not* made up of nuns (women), but consisted entirely of men. They were a "religious brotherhood." [140]

Blunder 2: Because Mary has her arm around one of the two babies, Dan Brown misinterprets the meaning and reads into the painting some hidden meaning. Mary has her arm around the larger of the two babies which would presumably be the older one—John the Baptist. In one of the two paintings, the larger child—John the Baptist—has his recognizable staff in his arms.

Blunder 3: It is inconceivable that any student of the Bible would place any stock in the value of a painting portraying Jesus as blessing while he was still a baby. This type of activity would certainly contradict what we see as the recorded examples of Jesus' early life. Each of them reveals that Mary lacked a complete understanding of exactly Who her Son was.

- The sayings of the shepherds in the manger made Mary contemplative.

  And all they that heard it wondered at those things which were told them by the shepherds. But **Mary** kept all these things, and **pondered them in her heart.** [141]

- Joseph and Mary were surprised at what was said about Jesus when they brought Him to the temple as a baby.

  And **Joseph and his mother marvelled** at those things which were spoken of him. [142]

---

[140] http://www.nationalgallery.org.uk/cgibin/WebObjects.dll/CollectionPublisher.woa/wa/content?contentName=GL_Confraternity
[141] Luke 2:18-19.
[142] Luke 2:33.

- Again, when Jesus was twelve they brought him to the temple. Mary hid the things said about Him in her heart.

And he said unto them, How is it that ye sought me? wist ye not that I must be about my Father's business? And they understood not the saying which he spake unto them. And he went down with them, and came to Nazareth, and was **subject unto them**: but **his mother kept all these sayings in her heart**. [143]

Notice that the word of God is careful to point out that Jesus was subject to Joseph and His mother. In each of the three cases Mary pondered or kept the sayings in her heart because she did not have a full realization of exactly Who Jesus was. Although it is true that her understanding was humanly limited, she was in the best position to grasp much of His future. Cautioning against improper emphasis upon Mary, should not lead the Bible student to ignore what she did understand.

We know that Mary understood (by communication from God Himself via angels,[144] prophetic utterances,[145] etc.) that the child in her womb was conceived by the Holy Spirit.[146] She knew his God given names[147] with their meanings. She knew that her son was the Son of God the Most High, heir to David's throne.[148] She knew that she was the mother of the Lord; that Jesus was the promised Christ, the fulfillment of the promise to Abraham.[149] She knew that her

---

[143] Luke 2:49-51.
[144] Luke 1:26.
[145] Matthew 1:2, Luke 1:42.
[146] Luke 1:35.
[147] Luke 1:31, 35, 2:21.
[148] Luke 1:32.
[149] Luke 1:55.

Son was a light to the Gentiles,[150] a great joy to all people; she witnessed the gentile Magi worship her young son with gifts and prostrations;[151] she knew that Jesus was appointed for the fall and rising of many in Israel,[152] a sign to be opposed, a revealer of hearts and that all this would pierce her own soul as a sword.[153] Mary probably knew Him better than anyone else. Unlike many other followers of Christ during His last days she followed Him all the way to Calvary.

Never did Mary withdraw her initial submission to God's will concerning her role in the Saviour's life and mission though it most assuredly cost her enormous pain as His earthly mother. In spite of her understanding, it remains unreasonable to paint Jesus as bestowing a blessing upon another infant when the Bible says that He did not begin performing miracles until He was thirty years old. [154]

---

[150] Luke 2:32.
[151] Matthew 1:11.
[152] Luke 2:34
[153] Luke 2:35.
[154] This beginning of miracles did Jesus in Cana of Galilee, and manifested forth his glory; and his disciples believed on him (John 2:11).

8

Who was Mary Magdalene?

Mary Magdalene was one of the women from whom Jesus cast out devils. Nowhere does the Bible indicate that she was married to Jesus or was a prostitute. Her introduction comes in Luke chapter 8.

> And it came to pass afterward, that he went throughout every city and village, preaching and shewing the glad tidings of the kingdom of God: and the twelve were with him, And certain **women, which had been healed of evil spirits** and infirmities, **Mary called Magdalene, out of whom went seven devils**, [155]

The confusion comes when people try to self-interpret the Bible. The anonymous sinner woman mentioned in the previous chapter,[156] who anointed Jesus' feet in the house of Simon the Pharisee, was assumed to be Miriam of Magdala. Yet, there is no definitive proof that this was Mary Magdalene. In fact, the proof is balanced against these two narratives describing the same person.

Dan Brown uses one of his characters in the book to spin the unfortunate interpretation by a pope into his conspiracy theory.

> "Magdalene was recast as a whore in order to erase evidence of her powerful family ties." [157]

---

[155] Luke 8:1-2.
[156] Read Luke 7:44.
[157] Brown, p. 249.

Problems like these emerge from hypothetical assumptions about the word of God. The false assumptions cause very real problems when someone in a position of authority uses them to publicly misspeak. In this case, a blunder during a sermon delivered by *Pope Gregory the Great* in 591 AD provided the fuel necessary for the conspiracy theorists to start the rumor mill churning. This was the first record of mentioning of Mary Magdalene as a prostitute. In spite of what Pope Gregory said, there was no reason to believe that Mary was a prostitute. The Bible simply does not refer to her as such.

In all likelihood, the notion of her being a prostitute was caused by confusion concerning passages in Luke chapters 7 and 8 combined with the Catholic Church's tradition of wanting to supply a name for everyone. *Time* magazine reveals the dilemma for the Catholic Church. After making the official pronouncement that Mary Magdalene was a prostitute, church officials had to admit 1,300 years later that Pope Gregory was wrong. Here are two quotes from *Time* magazine.

> The mix-up was made official by Pope Gregory the Great in 591: "She whom Luke calls the sinful woman, whom John calls Mary [of Bethany], we believe to be the Mary from whom seven devils were ejected according to Mark," Gregory declared in a sermon. That position became church teaching...
>
> Three decades ago, the Roman Catholic Church quietly admitted what critics had been saying for centuries: Magdalene's standard image as a reformed prostitute is not supported by the text of the Bible. [158]

---

[158] David Van Biema, *Time*, Mary Magdalene Saint or Sinner? A new wave of literature is cleaning up her reputation. How a woman of substance was "harlotized", August 11, 2003. http://www.danbrown.com/media/morenews/time.html

Who was Mary Magdalene?

Since Mary is not the prostitute as the Catholic Church proclaimed for thirteen centuries, who was she? First and foremost, she is the one from whom seven demons were cast out;[159] she was present to witness the horrors of the crucifixion;[160] she also accompanied those that buried the Lord;[161] with two other women she went to anoint the body of Jesus;[162] and finally she was the first person to witness the resurrected Christ in person. The following is the most prominent passage concerning Mary Magdalene.

> But **Mary** stood without at the sepulchre weeping: and as she wept, she stooped down, and looked into the sepulchre, And seeth two angels in white sitting, the one at the head, and the other at the feet, where the body of Jesus had lain. And they say unto her, Woman, why weepest thou? She saith unto them, Because they have taken away my Lord, and I know not where they have laid him. And when she had thus said, she turned herself back, and saw Jesus standing, and knew not that it was Jesus. Jesus saith unto her, Woman, why weepest thou? whom seekest thou? She, supposing him to be the gardener, saith unto him, Sir, if thou have borne him hence, tell me where thou hast laid him, and I will take him away. Jesus saith unto her, **Mary**. She turned herself, and saith unto him, Rabboni; which is to say, Master. Jesus saith unto her, Touch me not; for I am not yet ascended to my Father: but go to my brethren, and say unto them, I ascend unto my Father, and your Father; and to my God, and your God. **Mary Magdalene came and told the disciples that she had seen the Lord, and that he had spoken these things unto her.** [163]

---

[159] Read Luke 8:2.
[160] Read Matthew 27:55-56.
[161] Read Matthew 27:61.
[162] Read Mark 16:1.
[163] John 20:11-18.

Far from trashing Mary Magdalene's reputation or participating in a smear campaign, the Bible assigns to her one of the highest honors—the recipient of the announcement of Christ's Resurrection. This passage is also the only place in the New Testament that records Jesus and Mary Magdalene as having been alone together. It certainly does not sound like there is anything more than a disciple/Lord relationship here. The Lord simply used Mary Magdalene as the conduit to inform the disciples that He had risen from the dead as promised on the third day.

Dan Brown uses the Lord's unmarried state as a vehicle to spin a good mystery novel. The Lord was unmarried and certainly not the only unmarried leader in the first century churches. The Apostle Paul was single and encouraged others to stay that way because of the necessity to reach the Jews before God cut them off. He defended his right to marry. In his comments concerning his authority to marry, he certainly would have listed Jesus as his number one argument had Jesus been married. As the Apostle Paul defends his right to get married, he does not use Christ as the prime example or include Him at all in the list.

If, according to Dan Brown, the "social decorum during that time virtually forbid a Jewish man to be unmarried"[164] then why would Paul find it necessary to defend his right to marry rather than defending his decision to remain unmarried?

> Have we not power to lead about a sister, **a wife**, as well as other apostles, and as the brethren of the Lord, and Cephas? [165]

---

[164] Brown, p. 245.
[165] 1 Corinthians 9:5.

The Plot Thickens

Dan Brown sets forth Leonardo Da Vinci's painting of *The Last Supper* as further evidence of Jesus' alleged marriage to Mary Magdalene. He claims that Leonardo was a member of the Priory of Sion and hid codes in his paintings. However, none of Leonardo's fifteen manuscripts still in existence today reveal any involvement in the Priory of Sion.

Dan Brown claims that *The Last Supper* depicts Mary Magdalene and not John to Jesus' right side. While it is true that John looks effeminate in *The Last Supper*, this is similar to visual techniques used in other paintings by this artist and by other artists of the same period. Even John the Baptist was portrayed in a feminine way by Leonardo— although the Bible portrays him quite differently. "And the same John had his raiment of camel's hair, and a leathern girdle about his loins; and his meat was locusts and wild honey."[166] John the Baptist certainly would not seem very effeminate from this biblical depiction.

There is no evidence that Leonardo was a member of the Priory of Sion and no evidence that he meant for anyone to interpret his painting as including anyone other than those actually present at the Last Supper. "And he answered and said unto them, It is **one of the twelve**, that dippeth with me in the dish."[167]

Another plausible, yet unverifiable, reason for Leonardo's depiction of men with effeminate features and supposedly androgynous figures could relate to the artist's own sexual affiliation. Although Leonardo was never found guilty, he was charged with the crime of sodomy. It is just as reasonable to consider this aspect of the artist's past, as to allow Dan Brown to spin intricate tales as to why he chose to paint in this fashion.

---

[166] Matthew 3:4.
[167] Mark 14:20.

Art historian Bruce Boucher writing for *The New York Times* in 2003, "...despite a charge of sodomy against him as a young man, the evidence of his sexual orientation remains inconclusive and fragmentary." [168]

Yet, Dan Brown ignores this information and angle and continues to weave his plot even thicker. According to Dan Brown, Jesus...

"...gives Mary Magdalene instructions on how to carry on His Church after He is gone. As a result, Peter expresses his discontent over playing second fiddle to a woman. I daresay Peter was something of a sexist." [169]

Talk about rewriting all of history—Peter had many faults which the Bible never shies away from presenting. Now to this list we are to add that he was some sort of sexist because he had to play "second fiddle" to Jesus' supposed wife? The apostles would have lacked any type of character had they expected Jesus to place them in front of His supposed spouse.

Mary Magdalene—the Rock?
The Gnostics' worldview demands that their spiritual entities exist in male and female pairs. Therefore, it comes as no surprise that Mary Magdalene was chosen as the counterpart for Jesus. History has taught us that the more unbelievable the claim, the greater the chance of its acceptance. Brown proves this point with the following thought.

"The rock on which Jesus built His Church... was not **Peter**... It was **Mary Magdalene**."[170]

---

[168] *The New York Times*, August 3, 2003.
[169] Brown, pgs. 247-248.
[170] Brown, p. 248.

The joke continues.

> "Jesus was the original feminist. He intended for the future of His Church to be in the hands of Mary Magdalene." [171]

All of the femi-nazis shout hallelujah! Interestingly, Christ never said that Peter was to be the rock upon which He would build His church. In fact, He was going to build His church based on Peter's *confession* concerning His Deity. Peter confessed that *Jesus was* **the Christ.** This fact of Jesus' Deity would be the rock upon which the whole church would be built. This is also the very foundation so vehemently attacked by Dan Brown and Satan himself. Nothing should detract or distract from Christ—not Peter, Mary, Mary Magdalene or anyone else. The scriptures plainly say that Christ is the Rock.

> And did all drink the same spiritual drink: for they drank of that spiritual Rock that followed them: and **that Rock was Christ.** [172]

Christ is THE Rock. All of the apostles and prophets are the foundation of the church; however, Christ is the only One that is given a unique or prominent position among that group. He is the Rock and chief corner stone.

> And are built upon the foundation of the apostles and prophets, **Jesus Christ himself being the chief corner stone;** [173]

---

[171] Ibid.
[172] 1 Corinthians 9:5.
[173] Ephesians 2:20.

He is the one and only head of the church. Nobody took His place and nobody will take His place.

For the husband is the head of the wife, even as **Christ is the head of the church**: and he is the saviour of the body. [174]

Christ is the head of the body—the Church. He is to have the preeminence in all things.

And he **is the head of the body**, the church: who is the beginning, the firstborn from the dead; that **in all things he might have the preeminence**. [175]

According to *The American Heritage® Dictionary of the English Language*, preeminence means that one is "superior to or notable above all others; outstanding." [176] He is to be most prominent in all of our thoughts and endeavors.

Since Christ is to be superior to all others, it should not surprise us when everyone is always trying to steal the preeminence rightfully belonging to Him. Satan tried to accomplish this very endeavor in the temptation of Matthew chapter 4, as well as in the Garden of Eden. Any effort that attempts to steal Christ's preeminence is satanic in nature. The *Da Vinci Code* attempts to elevate Mary Magdalene and a "sacred sexual ceremony" above Christ. This ploy, too, is satanic.

---

[174] Ephesians 5:23.
[175] Colossians 1:18.
[176] The American Heritage® Dictionary of the English Language, Fourth Edition
Copyright © 2000 by Houghton Mifflin Company.

9

A Novel Celebrating Gross Immorality

The Da Vinci Code elevates fornication to some sort of two thousand year old sacred ceremony that supposedly allows a person to commune with God. No doubt this has helped the book to sell so well—people like a good plot that includes sex and intrigue.

> "For the early church...mankind's use of sex to commune directly with God posed a serious threat to the Catholic power base. It left the Church out of the loop, undermining their **self-proclaimed status as the sole conduit to God**. For obvious reasons, they worked hard to demonize sex and recast it as a disgusting and sinful act. Other major religions did the same."[177]

Of course, I do not believe that the Catholic Church is the sole conduit to God. And sex was never meant to be any such conduit either. We are to commune with God through prayer and other such spiritual activities as defined in the scripture.

> Be careful for nothing; but in every thing by prayer and supplication with thanksgiving let your requests be made known unto God. And the peace of God, which passeth all understanding, shall keep your hearts and minds through Christ Jesus. Finally, brethren, whatsoever things are true, whatsoever things are honest, whatsoever things are just, whatsoever things are pure, whatsoever things are lovely,

---

[177] Brown, p. 309.

whatsoever things are of good report; if there be any virtue, and if there be any praise, think on these things. [178]

Philippians tells us to *pray* and to *think* on those things which are true, honest, just, pure and lovely. Dan Brown's book certainly encourages otherwise. Essentially, Brown tells his readers that they should be thinking about sex since it is the act that enables one to "experience" God!

> "Historically, **intercourse was the act through which male and female experienced God**. The ancients believed that the male was spiritually incomplete until he had carnal knowledge of the sacred feminine. **Physical union with the female remained the sole means through which man could become spiritually complete and ultimately achieve gnosis**—knowledge of the divine." [179]

Christians are *complete* in Christ and do not need to partake in extra-marital sex or any sex whatsoever to be made spiritually complete. The Bible says that we are complete in Him.

> For in him dwelleth all the fulness of the Godhead bodily. And ye are **complete in him**, which is the head of all principality and power: [180]

Earlier in the book, Brown's key figure—the Harvard professor Langdon—mentions *Hieros Gamos* as the means to experience this higher level of spirituality. He does this after rightfully condemning the Catholic Inquisition witch

---

[178] Philippians 4:6-8.
[179] Brown., p. 308.
[180] Colossians 2:9-10

hunts. However, he glamorizes *Hieros Gamos* and proclaims it as necessary for spiritual enlightenment.

> "The once hallowed act of Hieros Gamos—the natural sexual union between man and woman through which each became spiritually whole—had been recast as a shameful act. **Holy men who had once required sexual union with their female counterparts to commune with God** now feared their natural sexual urges as the work of the devil, collaborating with his favorite accomplice...**woman**." [181]

The form of sex that Brown elevates in the book is in fact a form of eroticism. The man is to use his partner to fulfill his own sexual desire. It says nothing of the concern that the man is to have for his partner's fulfillment.

Hieros Gamos—(Greek: "sacred marriage") referred to sexual relations of fertility deities enacted in myths and rituals, characteristic of societies based on cereal agriculture (e.g., Mesopotamia and Phoenicia). A modern day example of a group that still engages in the ritual that Dan Brown seems to want revived is Wicca (witchcraft). [182]

At least once a year, people dressed as gods engaged in sexual intercourse to "guarantee" the fertility of the land. The festival began with a procession to the marriage celebration, which was followed by an exchange of gifts, a purification rite, the wedding feast, preparation of the wedding chamber and a secret nocturnal act of intercourse. [183]

Aleister Crowley

All of these symbols and rituals sound eerily similar to

---

[181] Brown, p. 125.
[182] http://en.wikipedia.org/wiki/Hieros_gamos
[183] Britannica Concise Encyclopedia. http://www.britannica.com/ebc/article-9367077?query=marriage&ct=

those of Aleister Crowley—the self-proclaimed "beast 666." In 1901, after practicing Raja Yoga for some time, Crowley claims to have reached a state he called *dhyana*. His new religious philosophy was simple: "Do what thou wilt shall be the whole of the law." He died in 1947 as a penniless heroin addict. He also believed that he was reincarnated from the eighteenth century occultist Count Cagliostro, Eliphas Levi (who died on the same day that Crowley was born).

During his day the British press labeled him "The Wickedest Man in the World," yet in 2002 he was voted in as one of the 100 "Greatest Britons" of all time showing that he still has considerable influence today.[184] Notice the similarities of *Hieros Gamos* glorified in *The Da Vinci Code* with the "Sex Magick" popularized by Aleister Crowley. According to Wikipedia.org, *Sex Magick* is thought to be the most powerful of all magick[185]:

> Sex Magick is the use of the sex act—or the energies, passions or arousal states it evokes—as a point upon which to focus the will or magical desire for effects in the non-sexual world. In this, Crowley was inspired by Paschal Beverly Randolph, an American author writing in the 1870s who wrote (in his book *Eulis!*) of using the "nuptive moment" (orgasm) as the time to make a "prayer" for events to occur. While Randolph was interested in both the male and female partners, **Crowley's version of sex magick was a male-centered activity and the female partner played a passive role.**[186]

Much like *Hieros Gamos*, it is the man that is satisfied through Sex Magick and the woman plays a passive role. In

---

[184] http://www.wordiq.com/definition/100_Greatest_Britons
[185] http://en.wikipedia.org/wiki/Sex_Magick
[186] http://www.reference.com/browse/wiki/Aleister_Crowley

order to complete the connective circle, the relationship should be made from Crowley to Rock-n-Roll groups and eventually to the highest office in the world—The President of the United States. These seemingly unrelated matters further reveal the depth of ignorance in the world today.

The Beatles placed Crowley on the album cover of *Sgt. Pepper's Lonely Hearts Club Band*. Michael Jackson's 1991 album *Dangerous* featured a drawing of Crowley on the cover. Many other Rock-n-Roll singers referenced Crowley in their lyrics—David Bowie, **Ozzy Osbourne**, Marilyn Manson and Led Zeppelin are a few examples. **Osbourne** released a song in his *Prince of Darkness* album (2005) entitled "Mr. Crowley":

> Mr. Crowley, what went on in your head?
> Oh, Mr. Crowley, did you talk with the dead?
> Your life style to me seemed so tragic
> With the thrill of it all
> You fooled all the people with magic.
> Yeah, you waited on satan's door.

Interestingly, President George Bush invited Ozzy Osbourne to the White House Correspondents Association Ball on May 4, 2002. The news reported: While dessert was being served Ozzy Osbourne, and wife Sharon, were urgently ushered to the stage rope line for a face to face with the Commander in Chief. This is what the President of the United States had to say to this reprobate that has deceived and condemned so many through his music and lifestyle. President Bush said, "The thing about Ozzy is, he's made a lot of big hit recordings: *Party With the Animals, Sabbath Bloody Sabbath, Face in Hell, Black Skies* and *Bloodbath in Paradise*. Ozzy, Mom loves your stuff." [Title should be *"Facing Hell"*] [187] Some will claim this is just politics, but look how far we have come.

---

[187] http://www.cuttingedge.org/News/n1758.cfm

As bad as this encounter was for a *conservative* President, it seems that the Bush administration was preceded by really weird influences in the Clinton administration too. Jean Houston is a close friend and counselor to Hilary Clinton. She served as the first lady's counselor in the 1990's while Hilary was first lady.

Jean Houston has many esoteric beliefs which would seem to reflect those held by Hilary Clinton too. Houston believes that society needs to be rebuilt under the goddess Isis and Osiris. The similarities to Dan Brown's teachings are easily identifiable. She interprets the Gnostic texts as teaching that Jesus is and will be partnered with a female figure—**Sophia**. Here are Jean Houston's own words:

> Later Gnostic texts present similar figures, the crucified Jesus being partnered again by his Beloved in Heaven, the Sophia who is the feminine wisdom of God." [188]

The **Watchman Fellowship** provides this profile of Jean Houston on their website:

> Her influence has reached even the White House. During numerous lengthy stays with Hilary Clinton, Houston has led the First Lady into guided imagery (meditation) sessions to contact and consult with Eleanor Roosevelt" (*Newsweek*, July 1, 1996, p. 26). ... Jean Houston was born in 1941...Houston's first grade teacher at a Catholic school so strongly disciplined her that it somehow led her to escape into a profound mystical experience, an eastern, pantheistic, monistic revelation (*New Age Encyclopedia*, p. 221; Jean Houston, *Possible Human*, pp. 185-187). ...

---

[188] Jean Houston, *The Passion of Isis and Osiris: A Gateway to Transcendent Love,* (New York: Ballantine Publishing Group, 1995) p. 247.

In the '60s Houston married Robert Masters, the psychotherapist and sexologist who co-authored the notorious Masters-Johnson report. Together they began to experiment with LSD and other hallucinogenic drugs, believing that the drug-induced altered states of consciousness "were most effective in conveying psychic truth to the participant," and "that authentic religious and mystical experiences occur among the drug subjects" (*New Age Encyclopedia,* p. 221).

Houston and her husband "also developed the ASCID (Altered States of Consciousness Induction Device) better known as 'the Witches Cradle,'" as it was believed to have been used by witches using sensory deprivation and movement to enhance "fantasies and alteration in consciousness" (*Encyclopedia of Occultism and Parapsychology,* p. 485).

When legal restrictions made hallucinogenic drug research more difficult, Houston and Masters began to focus on the use of meditation and guided imagery or visualization as an alternative technique for inducing altered states of consciousness. They hoped these techniques would facilitate the emergence of Man's fullest potential.

Melton observes that, "all of Houston's subsequent work has had its foundation in these ideas and the New Age notion of imminent planetwide transformation of the human race," (*New Age Encyclopedia,* p. 221) a reaching of a critical mass in consciousness (enough people with the New Age world-view, all thinking and feeling the right way), inaugurating a quantum leap into utopia....

Jean Houston has a New Age, occult view of reality. She

> describes her conversion experience as a young girl futilely trying to get the Virgin Mary to appear to her. Suddenly she had an experience she described as, "the key turned and the door to the universe opened." She and every aspect of nature, including the Virgin Mary, all "Became part of a single Unity" and it was all "very, very good" (*The Possible Human,* p. 186). [189]

These are the influencers of the most powerful people in the world. Dan Brown, like Hilary Clinton, has become enamored with this esoteric teaching. His sensationalist style of writing is influencing many people to question and doubt the truths that hold the only hope for society and the world.

The Da Vinci Code is nothing more than age-old pagan spirituality reintroduced and repackaged so that unwary fiction readers can become introduced to this teaching. The ultimate goal is complete indoctrination in this system of beliefs. Satan will use these tools to gain a stronghold in the spiritual warfare for the human soul. Goddess worship is simply nothing new. Jeremiah repeatedly warned the people against it thousands of years ago. They did not hearken to him then and they will not listen today. Here is one example of the futility of warning people against such things.

> As for the word that thou hast spoken unto us in the name of the LORD, we will not hearken unto thee. But **we will certainly do whatsoever thing goeth forth out of our own mouth, to burn incense unto the queen of heaven**, and to pour out drink offerings unto her, as we have done, we, and our fathers, our kings, and our princes, in the cities of Judah, and in the streets of Jerusalem: for then had we plenty of victuals, and were well, and saw no evil. [190]

---

[189] http://www.watchman.org/profile/hustnpro.htm
[190] Jeremiah 44:16-17.

Sex Advice from the Harvard Professor

Langdon recounts a lesson he taught at Harvard where he spoke on the subject of *Hieros Gamos*. He is asked by a student, *"Are you saying that instead of going to Chapel we should have more sex?"* [191]

No wonder this book is so popular, it mixes New Age mysticism while encouraging sexual promiscuity—all in the name of "God." This type of thinking appeals to the baser instincts of man. Here is Langdon's answer to the question of sex versus chapel.

> "Gentlemen...might I offer a suggestion for all of you. Without being so bold as to condone premarital sex...The next time you find yourself with a woman, look in your heart and see if you cannot approach sex as a mystical, spiritual act. Challenge yourself to find that spark of divinity that man can only achieve through union with the sacred feminine." [192]

In other words, Brown's fictitious character advises these students how to react "spiritually" the next time they find themselves confronted with an "opportunity" to engage in fornication. He advises them to just ignore all that the Bible teaches about marriage and purity. They are to repackage their sexual drives so that they can justify the sin by calling it something else.

Frankly, this book amounts to borderline pornography or at least a work that encourages sexual promiscuity among our youth. Langdon continues:

> "By communing with woman," Langdon said, "man

---

[191] Brown, p. 310.
[192] Ibid.

could achieve a climactic instant when his mind went totally blank and he could see God." [193]

This is just another Gnostic teaching. The Bible does not leave these things open to interpretation or opinion. Altered states of consciousness related to sexual promiscuity do not bring revelation or knowledge of God; they bring shame and disgrace. God's word alone is the supreme and infallible authority for everyone and a personal relationship with Him is the only way to know Him. Gnosis teaches that we are on a search to find Christ within all of us—it is done through self-awareness.

The Gnostics were those that blended Christian teachings with those of the Greek philosophers. They believed that their great knowledge would release them into the spiritual world after being freed from the physical world. Gnosticism taught salvation involved liberation of the spirit and that only the "enlightened" ones who possess the secret knowledge would rise to the level of God. [194]

The Gnostic teachings intermingled with the sexual promiscuity reveal that Dan Brown's moral compass must be spinning out of control. However, there is more. Brown depicts a couple copulating in the middle of many chanting people. Chanting is nothing new. The Bible describes the city of Ephesus as being totally influenced by the worship of the "great goddess Diana."

> Moreover ye see and hear, that not alone at Ephesus, but almost throughout all Asia, this **Paul hath persuaded** and turned away much people, **saying that they be no gods, which are made with hands:** So that not only this

---

[193] Brown, pgs. 308-309.

[194] Kerby F. Fannin, While Men Slept..., (Addison, MI: Life's Resources, Inc., 2002) p. 52-53.

our craft is in danger** to be set at nought; but also that the **temple of the great goddess Diana should be despised**, and her magnificence should be destroyed, **whom all Asia and the world worshippeth**. And when they heard these sayings, they were full of wrath, and cried out, saying, Great is Diana of the Ephesians. And **the whole city was filled with confusion**...[195]

Goddess worship is simply a form of devolution—or devolving into that which man left behind long ago. The whole city is filled with confusion. Today the goddess worshipers are attempting to take the world back to the first century when cities like Ephesus worshipped the goddess Diana. The book of Acts records that the chanting continued for about two hours until the town clerk appeased the mob:

But when they knew that he was a Jew, **all with one voice about the space of two hours cried out, Great is Diana of the Ephesians.** And when the townclerk had appeased the people, he said, Ye men of Ephesus, what man is there that knoweth not how that **the city of the Ephesians is a worshipper of the great goddess Diana**, and of the image which fell down from Jupiter? [196]

Chanting is nothing new and neither is achieving "gnosis" through sex with another person. It is simply another of the humanistic teachings illustrated in *The Da Vinci Code*. And it is simply another form of fornication condemned by God and His word.

God's natural design was for sex to take place between one man and one woman for reproduction and pleasure within the marriage relationship. Christianity has not recast

---

[195] Acts 19:26-29.
[196] Acts 19:34-35.

it as a shameful act. Sex within marriage is good and always has been. It is even required for a healthy relationship.[197] In fact, the Bible warns that prolonged abstinence can lead to satanic temptation.[198]

> **Defraud ye not one the other, except it be with consent for a time**, that ye may give yourselves to fasting and prayer; **and come together again, that Satan tempt you not for your incontinency.** [199]

Married couples are warned not to prolong their sexual abstinence lest their lack of intimacy unduly tempts them. They are told to quickly come together again after short periods of abstinence for fasting and prayer. Sex within the bounds of matrimony is normal, expected and encouraged. This sounds far from prudish, and it also does not sound like sex was ever intended to be a spiritual act to achieve "gnosis."

God created marriage from the very beginning and all sex outside of the marriage relationship is sinful. It actually places a barrier between the individual and God rather than some kind of spiritual union.

> **Marriage is honourable in all,** and the bed undefiled: but whoremongers and adulterers God will judge. [200]

The Bible has strong affirmations concerning the role of marriage. The husband and wife in the marriage relationship are partnering with God in the act of creation—the beginning

---

[197] Read Genesis 2:24; Matthew 19:5; 1 Corinthians 6:16; Ephesians 5:31.

[198] Maybe some of these men overcome with internet porn should begin to pay more attention to their wives and Satan will not tempt them as easily.

[199] 1 Corinthians 7:5.

[200] Hebrews 13:4.

of a new life. It comes as no surprise that it is best for two people to come together in the covenant of marriage in a pure state.

Basically, Brown asks us to believe that Christianity destroyed the woman's rightful position and that paganism attempts to restore her proper state. Yet, his book also degrades women by making them the mere objects of man's sexual pleasures. Furthermore, his book condones and encourages sexual promiscuity outside the marriage relationship, claiming that God ordained it. Historically, his way of thinking has been a way for men to fulfill their sexual lusts by demeaning and degrading women. It is interesting that there is not a word of complaint against this book originating from the so-called women's rights groups.

Heterosexual monogamy is the one flesh marriage of the Bible. It is the only security in sexual relations that exists. Multiple partners simply create confusion, insecurity and deep emotional pain eventually resulting in rejection and remorse. Women merely become a sexual tool to fulfill man's sexual desires.[201] This is why the Bible says that Christians are to abstain from fornication—defined as sex outside of marriage.

> But that we write unto them, that they **abstain from** pollutions of idols, and from **fornication**, and from things strangled, and from blood. [202]

> Meats for the belly, and the belly for meats: but God shall destroy both it and them. Now **the body is not for fornication**, but for the Lord; and the Lord for the body. [203]

The book of Acts says that everyone is to abstain from

---

[201] Shame on the husband that falls within this same parameter with his wife.
[202] Acts 15:20.
[203] 1 Corinthians 6:13.

fornication. The body is not for fornication and we are told to flee from it. It is a sin against one's own body.

> **Flee fornication.** Every sin that a man doeth is without the body; but he that committeth fornication sinneth against his own body. [204]

No matter the degree to which the Bible warns against extra-marital sex, the overwhelming popularity of the number one best seller on the *New York Times* best seller's list certainly reveals the sad moral state of society. *The Da Vinci Code* condones and encourages the very thing that the Bible warns against. For those that need one more obsessive tidbit, according to Dan Brown even the architecture has sexual connotations.

> On the back, Collet found notations scrawled in English, describing a cathedral's long hollow nave as a secret pagan tribute to a woman's womb. This was strange. The notations describing the cathedral's *doorway*, however, was what startled him. "Hold on! He thinks a cathedral's entrance represents a woman's..."
>
> The examiner nodded. "Complete with receding labial ridges and a nice little cinquefoil clitoris above the doorway." He sighed. "Kind of makes you want to go back to church." [205]

This proposition is quite hard to fathom. This would mean that centuries prior to the existence of these groups, the Priory of Sion and the Templars impacted the medieval architecture. Materials covering the architectural history of

---

[204] 1 Corinthians 6:18.
[205] Brown, p. 326.

these cathedrals reveal that the public basilicas and the ancient Greco-Roman world influenced the design of these structures—not some sensationalistic conspiracy.

Dan Brown's thoughts come through loud and clear with the following statement from the mouth of Langdon:

> "Our ancient heritage and our very physiologies tell us sex is natural—a cherished route to spiritual fulfillment—and yet modern religion decries it as shameful, teaching us to fear our sexual desire as the hand of the devil." [206]

Dan Brown is right about one thing—the sexual union between a man and woman is spiritual. However, God intended for this bond to be limited to marriage and not some secret ritual that functions as a way to commune with Him! Honest seekers of truth need to realize that denying one's sexual fulfillment until marriage is not prudish, but prudent. Abstinence before marriage allows the couple to come together and discover each other in ways that are neither sinful nor harmful. God intended it that way. Sex is holy and marriage is sacred, but man has perverted sex and maligned marriage. Dan Brown simply wants his cake and wants to eat it too. There is nothing new about his teaching. It is the same teaching that has toppled many great societies bringing them down because of their moral decay.

---

[206] Ibid., 310.

10

The Shirley MacLaine Connection

Brown has Langdon say that the *Mona Lisa* painted by Leonardo da Vinci was not really meant to represent a woman but was androgynous—neither male nor female. He even claims that her name was an anagram for the divine union between male and female.[207] Brown's theory is easily discredited. There is no record of Leonardo da Vinci's ever naming this painting in any of his writings or notebooks.

In fact, Giorgio Visari, Leonardo's first biographer, was the first to identify the portrait as the *Mona Lisa*. This biography was written 30 years after Leonardo's death so it is impossible for Leonardo to be communicating some hidden meaning through its title if the name did not even originate with him. Brown connects the supposed androgynous state of the *Mona Lisa* with the sex act witnessed by Sophie in the book.

Langdon asks Sophie whether the participants in the *Hieros Gamos* (the sexual ritual that she witnessed at the beginning of the story) were wearing *androgynous* masks while engaged in this ritual. She affirms that they were. [208]

Langdon goes on to explain that this sex ritual (although not a form of eroticism because it is defined as spiritual), was the way that man could commune with God. Langdon says, *"By communing with woman...man could achieve a climactic instant when his mind went totally blank and he could see God."* Sophie responds—*"Orgasm as prayer."* Langdon agrees that she is basically correct because the climax is accompanied by a *"split second entirely*

---

[207] Brown, p. 121.
[208] Ibid., 308.

void of thought. A brief mental vacuum." He goes on to explain that it was much like the meditation gurus' thoughtless state of Nirvana. [209]

The book encourages a mindless state sought by Saunière which is similar to Hindu and Buddhist meditation techniques. The chanting is a repetitious mantra used as a spiritual conduit which comes from two Sanskrit words. The root *man*— "manas or mind," and the suffix *-tra* meaning "tool" thus the literal translation would be "mind tool." Chanting is the process of repeating a mantra. [210]

Dan Brown's writings and ideas are nothing new. They are simply regurgitated and repackaged Shirley MacLaine philosophy. According to an advertisement for the audio tapes of her books, MacLaine gives her thoughts to the "spiritual seeker" seeking a "heightened awareness of one's inner self." Amazon.com describes the reading of her book onto audio cassette: *"reading in a clear, straightforward voice, the author's slow tones and careful stops at the end of each sentence help the listener focus on the inner self. MacLaine makes the practice of meditation easy as she lulls the listener into a trans-like state..."*[211]

Her book gives her thoughts on the purpose of life too. She believes and teaches that our purpose is to know ourselves as we truly are— "**androgynous**, a perfect balance." [212]

The connection between all of the various players is uncanny. *Hieros Gamos* replaces the normal and natural sex rite with a ritual sex orgy. In doing so, Brown cheapens God's perfect ways. He also extols the virtues of an androgynous state when God created two distinct genders—male and

---

[209] Ibid.

[210] http://www.reference.com/browse/wiki/Mantra

[211] http://www.amazon.com/gp/product/0553283316/ref=ed_oe_p/104-8214946-3835941?%5Fencoding=UTF8

[212] Shirley MacLaine, Going Within: A Guide for Inner Transformation, (New York: Bantam Books, 1989), 197.

female.[213] The repetitive nature found in these prayer chants is also warned against in the Bible as repetitious prayers.

> But when ye pray, use not vain repetitions, as the heathen do: for they think that they shall be heard for their much speaking.[214]

The Bible covers every chant and schism ever devised by man or Satan. Prayer is certainly communing with God, but man continually perverts God's ways. God wants prayer to emanate from the heart. Satan desires that prayer become ritualistic and hollow. Chanting fulfills Satan's ultimate desire to shift man's focus away from its intended target.

---

[213] See Genesis 1:27.
[214] Matthew 6:7.

11

Overview: Mary Magdalene & the Gnostic Gospels

Dan Brown mentions the Nag Hammadi texts found in Egypt. These thirteen codices found in 1945 near a fourth century monastery (St. Pachomius) contained largely Gnostic works. The following is a synopsis of how the Gnostic Gospels portray Mary Magdalene:

The Gospel of Thomas—see preceding text.

The Gospel of Peter—she only appears on Resurrection morning when the women come to the tomb. They run away frightened when the angel appears to them.

The Dialogue of the Savior—Has frequent dialog with Christ, but no hint of a marriage.

The Sophia of Jesus Christ—twice she asks questions of Christ.

The Pistis Sophia— Mary is praised in *The Pistis Sophia* as one *"whose heart is more directed to the Kingdom of Heaven than all [her] brothers"*.... Jesus says that she is *"blessed beyond all women upon the earth, because [she shall be] the pleroma of all Pleromas and the completion of all completions."*[215] In other words, Mary will have the fullness of knowledge and therefore spiritual life within her. So impressed is Jesus with Mary's spiritual excellence that He promises not to conceal anything from her, but to reveal everything to her

---

[215] (section 19)

"with certainty and openly."[216] She is the blessed one who will *"inherit the whole Kingdom of the Light."* [217]

It is from *The Pistis Sophia* that the interest in Mary Magdalene grows among Gnostics, who valued knowledge (*gnosis* in Greek) above all else. She has come to be regarded as a source of hidden revelation because of her supposed intimate relationship with Jesus. However, nothing in this gospel goes so far as to suggest a marriage between the two of them.

The Gospel of Mary— *The Gospel of Mary*, written in the second century, goes even further than *The Pistis Sophia* in portraying Mary as a source of secret revelation because of her supposed close relationship to the Lord. At one point Peter asks, *"Sister, We know that the Savior loved you more than the rest of women. Tell us the words of the Savior which you remember—which you know but we do not nor have we heard them"*....She is the recipient of his secret revelations and private speeches. The Savior, who is not called Jesus in *The Gospel of Mary*, even preferred Mary to the other disciples, loving her more than them. It is this gospel that places Mary's relationship with Jesus into a new dimension.

The Gospel of Philip—this is the last of the extra-biblical gospels to mention Mary Magdalene, and the one that excites proponents of her marriage to Jesus more than any other ancient document. Mary Magdalene, mentioned only twice within the document, plays a small part in this gospel.

The first of these passages reads, *"There were three who*

---

[216] (section 25).
[217] (section 61).

always walked with the Lord: Mary his mother and her sister and Magdalene, the one who was called his companion."[218] Much has been insinuated because of this so-called gospel. The word for "companion" in the Greek original of this gospel is *koinonos*. Contrary to what is taught, this word doesn't mean spouse or sexual consort. It means "partner," and is used several times in the New Testament with this ordinary meaning. For example, Paul refers to himself as Philemon's *koinonos* in the Philemon 17.

> Philemon 17 If thou count me therefore a **partner**, receive him as myself.

Elaine Pagels covers the Nag Hammadi Gnostic texts in her book, *Beyond Belief: The Secret Gospel of Thomas*. The Gnostic Society Library, in its introduction to the Nag Hammadi Library, writes the following: [219]

> In many of the Nag Hammadi Gnostic texts God is imaged as a dyad of masculine and feminine elements. Though their language is specifically Christian, Gnostic sources often use sexual symbolism to describe God. Prof. Pagels explains,

> One group of gnostic sources claims to have received a secret tradition from Jesus through James and through Mary Magdalene [who the Gnostics revered as consort to Jesus]. Members of this group prayed to both the divine Father and Mother:

> 'From Thee, Father, and through Thee, Mother, the two immortal names, Parents of the divine being, and thou,

---

[218] (section 59).
[219] http://www.webcom.com/gnosis/naghamm/nhlintro.html

dweller in heaven, humanity, of the mighty name...'[220]

Dan Brown says that the Gnostic Gospels support the sacred feminine. Here is a short excerpt from *The Dialogue of the Saviour*:

> Judas said, "You have told us this out of the mind of truth. When we pray, how should we pray?"
>
> The Lord said, "Pray in the place where there is no woman." Matthew said, "'Pray in the place where there is no woman,' he tells us, meaning 'Destroy the works of womanhood,' not because there is any other manner of birth, but because they will cease giving birth." [221]

Why are the very people proclaiming the virtues of feminism willing to turn a blind eye to this obvious sexism found in these texts? Their sole purpose is the perversion of truth and they are willing to ignore these indiscretions in order to make the Bible and Christianity appear chauvinistic.

---

[220] Elaine Pagels, *Beyond Belief: The Secret Gospel of Thomas* (New York, 2003), p. 49.

[221] http://www.webcom.com/gnosis/naghamm/dialog.html

12. Original Sin

Innate within every human being is the understanding that he falls short of the glory of God. This is why every man-made religion contains a system of works attempting to reconcile its disciples with the Maker (or some other manmade god). The problem is that all avenues to God are fruitless when man tries to reach Him on his own terms without first being reconciled through the shed blood of the cross of Calvary.

Those that listen to Dan Brown's teachings negate and destroy the whole foundation of the true Gospel. Christ became a man and died on the cross of Calvary for sinners. Dan Brown writes that man created the concept of *original sin* and implies that the Bible teaches that Eve "caused the downfall of the human race" making her the enemy of Christianity.

> It was **man**, not God, who created the concept of 'original sin,' whereby Eve tasted of the apple and caused the downfall of the human race. Woman, once the sacred giver of life, was now the enemy. [222]

Christians and the Bible in general are not misogynistic—haters of women. In other words, there is no inherent hatred for women in the Bible or in true Christian teachings and doctrine.

Furthermore, Dan Brown's position is simply a misrepresentation of what the Bible says and what Christianity teaches concerning how sin came into the world. The Bible does *not* say that *by one woman* sin entered into the world. It says that it was by one *man*!

---

[222] Brown, p. 238.

Wherefore, as **by one man sin entered into the world**, and death by sin; and so death passed upon all men, for that all have sinned: [223]

In order to further realize the ridiculousness of Dan Brown's position, the full context of the passage is provided herein. The remainder of the passage refers to *Adam's transgression...the offence of one...one that sinned...one man's offence... and one man's disobedience*. So much for Brown's hypothesis that the Bible or Christianity teaches that Eve caused the downfall of the human race.

(For until the law sin was in the world: but sin is not imputed when there is no law. 14 Nevertheless death reigned from Adam to Moses, even over them that had not sinned after **the similitude of Adam's transgression**, who is the figure of him that was to come. But not as the offence, so also is the free gift. For if through **the offence of one** many be dead, much more the grace of God, and the gift by grace, which is by one man, Jesus Christ, hath abounded unto many. And not as it was **by one that sinned**, so is the gift: for the judgment was by one to condemnation, but the free gift is of many offences unto justification. For if **by one man's offence death reigned by one**; much more they which receive abundance of grace and of the gift of righteousness shall reign in life by one, Jesus Christ.) Therefore as **by the offence of one** judgment came upon all men to condemnation; even so by the righteousness of one the free gift came upon all men unto justification of life. For as **by one man's disobedience** many were made sinners, so by the obedience of one shall many be made righteous.[224]

---

[223] Romans 5:12.
[224] Romans 5:13-19.

It is true that Eve was the first to eat of the fruit, but sin entered the world when Adam partook of the forbidden tree. Eve was deceived,[225] but Adam willfully chose to sin against God. He chose to place God's creation above his Creator. Had he chosen not to follow Eve in eating the fruit, sin would not have entered the world. Eve would have died alone and Adam would have remained in a sinless state. Before blaming Adam, most every man put into the same position would probably have done the same thing.

However, the story thankfully does not end there. Through His infinite love, the same God that created man with a free will also provided the way for man to be reconciled to Himself. God became a man so that He could die for the very sins that Adam brought upon all future generations. But God could not die because He was sinless and the wages of sin is death; therefore, He had to take our sin upon Himself thus also taking upon Himself the wrath and righteous judgment of Almighty God.

> Now then we are ambassadors for Christ, as though God did beseech you by us: we pray you in Christ's stead, be ye reconciled to God. **For he hath made him to be sin for us**, who knew no sin; that we might be made the righteousness of God in him. [226]

Sinful man must first be changed in order to be reconciled to a holy, infinite God. Christ became sin—he took upon Himself the responsibility and the punishment for our sin thus making Him the one true and unique Saviour. In place of our sin, He gives us His perfect righteousness. It is a common misconception for people to claim to be Christians simply because they are not atheistic, Jewish, Muslim, Buddhist or Hindu.

---

[225] See 1 Timothy 2:14.
[226] 2 Corinthians 5:20-21.

A Christian is one who has made a conscious personal decision to accept the payment for sin made by Jesus Christ on his or her behalf. Christ died in vain if it is not the grace of God which brings salvation as a free gift.

> I do not frustrate the grace of God: for if righteousness come by the law, then Christ is dead in vain. [227]

> For by grace are ye saved through faith; and that not of yourselves: it is the gift of God: Not of works, lest any man should boast. [228]

The world seems balanced on the precipice of hell. As time continues, the Bible gives a description of the evil workers who will wax worse and worse until finally the world slides off into oblivion. "This know also, that in the last days perilous times shall come..."[229]

> But evil men and seducers shall wax worse and worse, deceiving, and being deceived. But continue thou in the things which thou hast learned and hast been assured of, knowing of whom thou hast learned them; And that from a child thou hast known the holy scriptures, which are able to make thee wise unto salvation through faith which is in Christ Jesus. [230]

---

[227] Galatians 2:21.
[228] Ephesians 2:8-9.
[229] 2 Timothy 3:1.
[230] 2 Timothy 3:13-15.

Addendum

The popularity of books and movies like *The Da Vinci Code* demonstrate Hollywood's influence over the world today. Its acceptance is another satanic "victory" in a long list of achievements profoundly affecting those duped by its message. Although the Bible foretells of Christ's ultimate victory, the battle between good and evil rages on.

The battle between Hollywood and the church can be likened to a spiritual chess match. However, the game is fixed by the god of this world.[231] Every move by the church is carefully scrutinized and unfairly characterized. As each side takes a turn, the church remains perpetually locked in "check." Each maneuver by the movie making industry is calculated in order to keep the church back on its heels. Any acceptance of their position by the church reveals a further weakening of the moral fiber. Those who attempt to defend a righteous position are looked upon contemptibly by those who think that the church must remain silent else they be viewed as unloving.

A movie depicting this century's most famous Christian martyrs is a case in point. The producers of the movie hired an activist homosexual to star in this supposed Christian flick. The church's silence condones this abhorrent lifestyle. Any attempt to accurately characterize the disdain for such a move plays to the media's portrayal of the church as unloving and hypocritical.

Homosexual Activist Stars in *The End of the Spear* Movie

Satan's spiritual arsenal leveled against Christians continues

---

[231] See 2 Corinthians 4:4.

to expand. One of his newest and most effective weapons is the so-called Christian movie. Through slick Hollywood advertising campaigns Christians are being convinced to pack the theaters in support of these supposed Christian films. Satan's most recent deception in this area revolves around the promotion and overwhelming acceptance by Christians of the recently released movie—*The End of the Spear*.

At no time in recent history could a brazenly activist homosexual star in a movie about a Christian martyr. Yet, this very thing is happening with Christians naïvely disputing the issue as though it were open to debate. This movie's producers who chose to eliminate the Gospel and Jesus Christ from the story also chose to include a homosexual activist to portray the man who epitomized the pinnacle of Christian commitment and sacrifice. The actor's chosen lifestyle disqualifies his involvement in this potentially worthy endeavor, invalidating any Christian support for this film. Choosing him to play the part dishonors the Lord and disgraces all those that have lived and died for Him.

The Story Behind the Story

January 8, 2006, marked the fiftieth anniversary of the death of five missionaries in Ecuador—Jim Elliot, Nate Saint, Peter Fleming, Ed McCully, and Roger Youderian. They were martyred on a sandy beach along the Curaray River by Ecuadorian natives. Their story 50 years ago shocked the entire world and had a reviving effect on worldwide missions. In fact, *Life* magazine chronicled the events as its cover story, dedicating ten pages to the tragedy.

Regretfully, the movie making machinery has cast a dark shadow on the legacy of these valiant men. **Every Tribe Entertainment** recently released its film about the missionaries focusing on Nate and Steve Saint—father and son. The conspicuous absence of both the Gospel and of Jesus Christ from the *The End of the Spear* is indicative of an industry attempting to please everyone except the impassioned Christian desiring the whole truth to be told.

The movie basically depicts a group of clean-cut white men going far out of their way to reach out to a group of cut-throat savages. The end of the story shows that these men sacrificed their lives in order to facilitate the savages' reform into clean-cut people too. Those unfamiliar with the true story could just as easily assume from the script of the movie that these missionaries were Mormons, rather than evangelical missionaries obediently fulfilling the Great Commission.

Another equally troubling aspect of the film is the casting of an openly activist homosexual in the star role. Chad Allen, a homosexual actor and activist, was chosen by Every Tribe Entertainment to play the starring role of missionary pilot Nate Saint, and that of his son Steve Saint. Every Christian should be concerned because Allen is an advocate for an anti-biblical, despicable lifestyle. Here is a man starring in a "Christian" themed movie that is not merely a sinful actor playing a part, but one that loves his sin and uses his fame to try to convince others of its legitimacy. Shamefully, Christian support of this film will provide him with a broader platform to further influence others concerning this deviant and perverse lifestyle.

Who is Chad Allen?

The man that plays the part of Nate Saint, the slain missionary is promoting the acceptance of homosexuality as natural, normal, and healthy. Granted, Christians should not expect the unregenerate to act any better than they do; however, our mission to reach the lost soul must never displace basic moral principles in the process.

In 2001, Allen produced and starred in a play that blasphemously paralleled the story of Christ. It is entitled **Corpus Christi**. It features a hard-drinking homosexual man named Joshua as the Christ-figure. After growing up isolated and ridiculed because of his homosexuality, Joshua flees the city and gathers a group of twelve disciples who cling to him because of "his message of love and tolerance." To further enforce the blasphemous connection of his Christ-like figure, most of Joshua's twelve so-called disciples bear the names of Christ's apostles.

In 2003, Allen started his own production company named Mythgarden in order to help produce shows that positively reflect homosexuality. He believes that it is time homosexuals are portrayed in "good relationships, real relationships, honest characters, in all of the genres of storytelling—fantasy, fiction, fairy tales, great mysteries, adventure films, and honest drama."[232]

In a Larry King Live[233] interview, Chad Allen attributed his homosexual lifestyle to God or a god. His interview reveals that his god is one of his own making. Allen told Larry King and the CNN audience:

> I have a deep relationship with [the] god of my understanding. It's very powerful, and it's taken its own shape and form. And I am very much at peace in the knowledge that in my heart god created this beautiful expression of my love. (meaning that God made him a homosexual)

Most of Allen's performances revolve around homosexuality. However, *The End of the Spear* allows him to change character and be viewed as a clean-cut man with the highest of moral standards.

It should matter to Christians who represents us to the world at large. This type of casting further confuses and blurs right and wrong in an already confused world on the brink of moral collapse. Chad Allen's fan base will certainly expand—

---

[232] http://www.chadallenonline.com/bio/bio2.html
[233] http://transcripts.cnn.com/TRANSCRIPTS/0601/17/lkl.01.html

especially amongst Christian children. His homosexuality while acting the part of a committed Christian who gave his life for the cause of Christ is irreconcilable.

Steve Saint's Blunder

Steve Saint, the son of the slain pilot, helped produce the film. He said that he recalled being shocked the first time he learned of Allen's homosexual lifestyle. Saint said that "upon further reflection he began to see the (homosexual) actor's involvement as possibly God-ordained." [234]

Three months after being hired, Allen offered to "walk away" from the contract; however, Steve Saint refused his offer. Saint said that God had spoken to him in a dream and warned him that having a homosexual play the part was the divine plan and that Saint should not worry about the Christians who would oppose the movie for that reason.

In his dream, he was chased by a mob of Christians who were angry with him for desecrating their story. Saint said he then heard God say, "'Steve, you of all people should know that I love all of my children. With regard to Chad Allen, I went to great lengths to orchestrate an opportunity for him to see what it would be like for him to walk the trail that I marked for him. Why did you mess with my plans for him?'"[235] The biggest problem with this scenario is that our dreams were never intended to be our guiding "light" in spiritual matters today. Including a homosexual because of a dream is bad enough, but excluding the Gospel and Jesus Christ in order to have a wider audience invalidates calling

---

[234] Jenni Parker, "Saint Defends Casting of Homosexual Actor in Christian Missionary's Story Slain," American Family Association Online,
http://headlines.agapepress.org/archive/1/192006b.asp

[235] Mark Moring, "Christian Studio Explains Hiring of Gay Actor," *Christianity Today*, 1/26/06,
http://www.christianitytoday.com/movies/news/chadallen.html

this a Christian film.

When Saint was confronted with the fact that the Gospel was not overtly present in the film, he responded. "The theater is not a good venue for doing that." Instead of going to hear preaching, he explains, "People go into the theater and they open up their 'cultural heart'—and that's where **new trends** in our society start; they start in the theater."[236]

There is only one "new trend" developing when an openly homosexual activist has the starring role in a movie about dedicated Christians having paid the ultimate sacrifice—acceptance for a lifestyle that the Bible condemns.

The Christian message and the messenger are intricately interwoven. It is completely unacceptable for an openly vocal homosexual messenger to *act* the part of a dedicated Christian. Can anything be more confusing? Dedicated Christians certainly do not openly and knowingly parade their sin for the world to see. Sin in one's life is a shameful thing which should never be legitimized.

The End Times Battle Lines are Being Drawn

Christians can well attest to the fact that Hollywood has never been a friend to Christianity. For decades now, Satan has instigated and effectively used the gross immorality coming out of Hollywood to adversely influence Christians. Fortunately, many Christians have withstood Satan's frontal assault upon everything decent. However, his use of moral compromise and spiritual infidelity seems to be effectively misleading those not seduced by his direct assault.

Allen's Website

Chad Allen's website[237] offers enough information for

---

[236] Ibid.

[237] Chad Allen's website (warning: foul language), http://www.chadallenonline.com/bio/index.html

anyone desiring to know who and what he is. The website clearly reveals the confusing environment in which Hollywood child idols are raised. Like many of these rising stars, Allen also struggled with alcohol and drugs—along with his homosexuality. He mentions that he was a popular teen idol with "a mega publicist who put out an image of me that seemed ideal." He mentions the teen magazines as portraying him as a perfect teenager. He says, "I was in teen magazines all the time and in reality, what was I? A 13-year-old who's as ——— up as every other 13-year-old across the country." Of course, his views of all teens were skewed by the environment in which he was raised. (expletive deleted)

According to Allen's website, "Courageously, in the October 9, 2001, issue of *The Advocate*, Chad came out as a gay man. He also acknowledged past problems with drugs and alcohol." He has been on the Cover of *The Advocate*—the leading homosexual magazine—at least three times.

In 2003, Allen started a company called Mythgarden. His stated goal is to use Mythgarden to show homosexual people in a positive light. Their motto is to push the "gay is good" theme. He is using this company to produce a television biography series about homosexual men and women he calls "heroes throughout history." He also has a series that takes classic fairy tales and gives them a homosexual twist. In fact, his company has optioned a book called *Fairy Tales for Gay Men*.

On Allen's website he reflects upon the first time he read the new fairy tale book. "When I read it for the first time, I found myself in a really nasty situation with my boyfriend at the time. We were breaking up and I turned to him and blurted out, 'What you want is not my idea of happily ever (after).'" [238]

The company's first play entitled *Save Me* is in pre-production and takes issue with **Reparative Therapy** methods

---

[238] http://www.chadallenonline.com/press/scene.htm

that are designed to help homosexuals change their chosen *lifestyle* (homosexual buzzword—*orientation*). Allen's website also reveals his vision behind Mythgarden. Allen says,

> Our company is entirely dedicated to turning the page on gay and lesbian storytelling in film, television, and theatre. We believe that it's time that our stories can be told fully: good relationships, real relationships, honest characters, in all of the genres of storytelling-fantasy, fiction, fairy tales, great mysteries, adventure films, and honest drama.[239]

Allen's website continues into 2004/2005:

> Chad continues to focus on his acting, and landed two very important roles in his career. One dual part in the highly anticipated film *End of the Spear*, which brought Chad on location all the way to South America, to film one of the greatest stories of forgiveness. The story was born from the death of five missionaries, led by Jim Elliot and Nate Saint. In January 2006, 50 years after the spearing, the feature length movie will release in theaters nationwide.[240]

> The other part was as Donald Strachey, in *Third Man Out*. **Here-TV**, a gay and lesbian television network, approached Chad with the detective story written by Richard Stevenson, and Chad signed on to do 6 movies in the Donald Strachey Mystery Series.[241]

---

[239] http://www.chadallenonline.com/bio/bio2.html
[240] Ibid.
[241] Ibid.

In 2004 he stepped back on the set of *NYPD Blue* for a second time, and delivered a powerful performance of a robber who picks up gay men, and ends up murdering one of his victims.[242]

Most of Allen's performances revolve around homosexuality. However, *The End of the Spear* allows him to change character and be viewed as a clean-cut man with the highest of moral standards. Utter confusion! "For God is not the author of confusion, but of peace, as in all churches of the saints." [243]

Contrary to Allen's spin on his website, he did not "courageously" come out of the closet in 2001. The first paragraph of the October 9, 2001, issue of *The Advocate* magazine, reveals that "somebody took a picture of him kissing a young man in the pool at that party, and some weeks later the tabloids outed him with that picture." The byline for the story reads: "The former teen idol and current actor-producer-activist tells all about his 1996 tabloid outing, his circuit party days, and his road to self-acceptance."[244] According to this 2001 article, Allen "came clean" five years after he had been "outed" by the tabloids in 1996 when the man whom he was kissing sold the picture. His public admission does not sound like a courageous move, but a calculated attempt to spin the story in his favor.

Allen's interview with the homosexual magazine clearly reveals the total identity confusion. He knew how to act, but not how to be himself or who he was:

---

[242] Ibid.
[243] 1 Corinthians 14:33.
[244] Bruce Vilanch, "Chad Allen: His Own Story," *The Advocate*, October 9, 2001. http://www.chadallenonline.com/press/advocate.htm

> I can get up in front of how many people every night onstage and be somebody else, but to sit here and be myself, I don't know who that is. ....I have been doing it since I was a kid. You think I'd know by now... Basically, I had been raised on the set and at church—strict Catholic upbringing there.[245]

Allen is asked, "**How strict was the Catholic upbringing?**" He answers: "Oh, heavy. When I wasn't working that was it, for 12 years. Of course, we didn't have nuns by the time I was in Catholic school." Allen is asked, "**Gay priests?**" "Sure. Some of them were very open. One was very open and helpful to students who were openly gay." "**Like you?**" "Like me. There was love and acceptance, and it was OK; they just weren't allowed to have sex. That was not my situation. I had to strike out and try everything on the great spiritual journey. Basically, I was having a blast in high school. It was the first time I had been off the set since I was 4 years old."[246]

The interview continues: "**Not so long ago you had a big reputation around drugs and parties. Were you a circuit boy?**" Allen responded,

> No, I was a guy who loved to push everything to its limits. That included the use of drugs and alcohol to expand and heighten every emotion to its absolute extreme. I've experienced the rave scene, the underground New York and L.A. scenes, the circuit party scene among gay men—all of it....I've had beautiful, intense romantic relationships with women in my life. And in this period in my life I have beautiful, intense romantic relationships with men.[247]

---

[245] Ibid.
[246] Ibid.
[247] Ibid.

Chad Allen's Homosexual Agenda

As reported in the Sharper Iron website, Allen was asked about his first gay (homosexual) love scene in a movie by an interviewer with *InLA* magazine. He responded, "I want beautiful, positive representations of gay male sexuality out there. So it was very important to the director, Ron Oliver, and me to make a really good sex scene that wasn't gratuitous or gross but was healthy, sexy, and beautiful."[248]

Allen stated in another interview with *InLA* magazine that he believed the *Spear* movie would bridge the gap between the "gay and Christian communities." Allen's homosexual agenda is quite clear:

> He is attempting to recast homosexuals in a positive light
> He is fighting for legal recognition of homosexual marriages
> He wants tolerance, acceptance and recognition of the homosexual lifestyle and agenda
> He gives generously to the "Gay and Lesbian Victory Fund" which helps elect openly homosexual candidates to public office

In another interview, Allen stated: "I want to be responsible for putting a committed loving fun gay relationship on TV so that those who are watching if they're young or old or in a relationship or not want to look up to this couple." [249]

Allen speaks of bridging the gap between homosexuals and Christians. Only *the Gospel of the Grace of God* and Allen's coming to a saving knowledge of Jesus Christ can bring this homosexual over to Christianity. Compromise and acceptance of his chosen lifestyle is completely out of the question. Any acceptance of this sinful lifestyle leavens the truth of

---

[248] http://www.sharperiron.org/showthread.php?t=2244Sharper%20Iron
[249] http://www.chadallenonline.com/press/scene.htm

Christianity and the regenerating power of its influence to change the sinner.

Chad Allen's god (expanded)

The root of Allen's confusion comes through time and again—especially during his appearance on *Larry King Live*. Chad Allen's god is not the God of the Bible. His interview on Larry King Live[250] reveals that his god is one of his own making. Allen told Larry King and the CNN audience:

> I have a deep relationship with [the] god of my understanding. It's very powerful, and it's taken its own shape and form. And I am very much at peace in the knowledge that in my heart god created this beautiful expression of my love.
>
> These days I judge all of my actions by my relationship with [the] god of my understanding. It is a deep-founded, faith-based belief in god based upon the work that I've done growing up as a Catholic boy and then reaching out to Buddhism philosophy, to Hindu philosophy, to Native American beliefs and finally as I got through my course with addiction and alcoholism and finding a higher power that worked for me.

Later in the *Larry King Live* program, Allen was asked about his involvement with *The End of the Spear* movie. He replied,

> I play a Christian, yes. And they're going to be saying, 'This is the way you be Christian, there's only one way.' Well you know what, there isn't. I'm a part of a wonderful community church here in Pasadena that has a very different interpretation of those same gospels that they are

---

[250] http://transcripts.cnn.com/TRANSCRIPTS/0601/17/lkl.01.html

speaking of. There isn't just one way to do this, there are a lot of paths.

What does the Bible say about Chad Allen's speculative multi-path route to heaven? Regretfully, it will eventually lead him and all of his entourage straight to hell. I would hate to be one of those responsible for giving him a greater opportunity through this film to tell others about his god, rather than the one true God.

> Enter ye in at the strait gate: for wide is the gate, and broad is the way, that leadeth to destruction, and many there be which go in thereat: Because strait is the gate, and narrow is the way, which leadeth unto life, and few there be that find it.[251]

Chad Allen's Buddhist, Hindu, Native American philosophical religion topped off with the god of his own understanding will not lead him to the truth. It is simply the broad way leading one to hell. He will have to reject these false gods and turn completely around (repent) to see the one and only true God who died for his sins on the cross of Calvary and awaits his acknowledgement of such. The Bible says there is only one way and that salvation revolves around that one Man—Christ Jesus.

> Jesus saith unto him, I am the way, the truth, and the life: no man cometh unto the Father, but by me.[252]

> Neither is there salvation in any other: for there is none other name under heaven given among men, whereby we must be saved.[253]

---

[251] Matthew 7:13-14.
[252] John 14:6.
[253] Acts 4:12.

Ever increasingly, Christians are more ignorant of Satan's devices and overtaken through his deceitful ways. The Christian message and the messenger are intricately interwoven. It is completely unacceptable for an openly vocal homosexual messenger to act like a dedicated Christian. Can anything be more confusing? These mixed signals are called the wiles of the Devil (Ephesians 6:11). The Bible also tells us that we are not ignorant of his devices (2 Corinthians 2:11).

Christians are being lulled into the world's way of thinking. Television and the movie industry are powerful forces reshaping our entire world. Hollywood has never been a friend to Christianity and will continue to reshape the world to fit Satan's design. A.W. Tozer (1897-1963) in his book, "On Worship and Entertainment: The Menace of the Religious Movie," hits the nail on the head almost prophetically describing the downward spiral witnessed today:

> Those who would appeal for precedent to the Miracle Plays have certainly overlooked some important facts. For instance, the vogue of the Miracle Play coincided exactly with the most dismally corrupt period the Church has ever known. When the Church emerged at last from its long moral night these plays lost popularity and finally passed away. And be it remembered, the instrument God used to bring the Church out of the darkness was not drama; it was the biblical one of Spirit-baptized preaching. Serious-minded men thundered the truth and the people turned to God. Indeed, history will show that no spiritual advance, no revival, no upsurge of spiritual life has ever been associated with acting in any form. The Holy Spirit never honors pretense.
>
> One thing may bother some earnest souls: why so many good people approve the religious movie. The list of those who are enthusiastic about it includes many who cannot be written off as borderline Christians. If it is an

evil, why have not these denounced it?

The answer is lack of spiritual discernment. Many who are turning to the movie are the same who have, by direct teaching or by neglect, discredited the work of the Holy Spirit. They have apologized for the Spirit and so hedged Him in by their unbelief that it has amounted to an out-and-out repudiation. Now we are paying the price for our folly. The light has gone out and good men are forced to stumble around in the darkness of the human intellect.

The religious movie is at present undergoing a period of gestation and seems about to swarm over the churches like a cloud of locusts out of the earth. The figure is accurate; they are coming from below, not from above. The whole modern psychology has been prepared for this invasion of insects. The fundamentalists have become weary of manna and are longing for red flesh. What they are getting is a sorry substitute for the lusty and uninhibited pleasures of the world, but I suppose it is better than nothing, and it saves face by pretending to be spiritual. Let us not for the sake of peace keep still while men without spiritual insight dictate the diet upon which God's children shall feed. [255]

Christians enticed to accept Satan's form of entertainment in the name of Christ will be increasingly influenced by a message that erodes the truths of scripture. The Christian movie phenomenon has only just begun—buckle your seatbelts because we are in for a very bumpy ride down a path as yet uncharted.

---

[254] A.W. Tozer, *On Worship and Entertainment: The Menace of the Religious Movie,* http://www.biblebb.com/files/tozermovie.htm

Bibliography

The American Heritage® Dictionary of the English Language, Fourth Edition Copyright © 2000 by Houghton Mifflin Company.

Barnes, Timothy D., Constantine and Eusebius, (Harvard: Presidents and Fellows of Harvard College, 1981).

THE BIBLICAL WORLD, ed. Charles F. Pfeiffer (Grand Rapids: Baker Book House, 1976),

Boyd, Gregory, Jesus Under Siege (Wheaton, IL: Victor, 1995).

Britannica Concise Encyclopedia. http://www.britannica.com/ebc/article-9367077?query=marriage&ct

Brown, Dan, Angels and Demons, (New York: Pocket Books, 2000).

_____, The Da Vinci Code (New York: Doubleday, 2003).

Eusebius, The History of the Church from Christ to Constantine, translated by G.S. Williamson, (Harmondsworth, Middlesex, England: Penguin Books, 1983).

Fannin, Kerby F., While Men Slept..., (Addison, MI: Life's Resources, Inc., 2002).

Garlow, James and Peter Jones, Cracking Da Vinci's Code (Colorado Springs, CO: Cook Communications, 2004).

Gleghorn, Michael, "Decoding the Da Vinci Code," www.probe.org.

Goldberg, Steven, Why Men Rule: A Theory of Male Dominance, (New York, NY: Open Court Publishing Co., 1994).

Grant, Robert M., The Formation of the New Testament (Harper and Row, 1965).

Hindson, Dr. Edward, National Liberty Journal, "Is God a Woman?"

Houston, Jean, The Passion of Isis and Osiris: A Gateway to Transcendent Love, (New York: Ballantine Publishing Group, 1995)

Introvigne, Di Massimo, "Beyond 'The Da Vinci Code': What is the Priory of Sion?" Center for Studies on New Religions. http://www.cesnur.org/2004/mi_davinci_en.htm

Irenaeus, ADVERSUS HAERESES, i.20.1.

MacLaine, Shirley, Going Within: A Guide for Inner Transformation, (New York: Bantam Books, 1989).

Miller, Laura, "The Last Word; The Da Vinci Con," The New York Times, February 22, 2004.

Moring, Mark, "Christian Studio Explains Hiring of Gay Actor," Christianity Today, 1/26/06, http://www.christianitytoday.com/movies/news/chadallen.html

THE NAG HAMMADI LIBRARY, ed. James M. Robinson (San Francisco: Harper & Row Publishers, 1978), p. 118.

Pagels, Elaine, Beyond Belief: The Secret Gospel of Thomas (New York, 2003),

TEACHINGS OF SILVANUS, 85.24-106.14, in NAG HAMMADI LIBRARY, pp. 347-56; cited by Pagels, GNOSTIC GOSPELS (New York: Random House, 1979).

Time Magazine, April 11, 2005, "The Novel that Ate the World," Michelle Orecklin
HYPERLINK
"http://www.danbrown.com/media/morenews/time041505.htm"
http://www.danbrown.com/media/morenews/time041505.htm
http://www.time.com/time/press_releases/article/0,8599,1047355,00.html

The Today Show, NBC, June 9, 2003, Dan Brown interview by Matt Lauer.
http://www.danbrown.com/media/todayshow.htm

Tozer, A.W., On Worship and Entertainment: The Menace of the Religious Movie,
http://www.biblebb.com/files/tozermovie.htm

The New York Times, August 3, 2003.

More Information

Dr. Douglas D. Stauffer has written six books and produced seven DVDs/videos on numerous biblical topics. His most recent books include:

The Da Vinci Con (124 page paperback) includes companion DVD or VHS
The Chronicles of Narnia: Wholesome Entertainment or Gateway to Paganism? (240 page paperback)
One Book Stands Alone (434 page hardback) includes 4-set companion DVDs or VHS

Other DVD/VHS exposés include:

Mel Gibson's Passion—A Biblical Analysis (dual DVD set)
Harry Potter—Innocent Entertainment? or Darkness Disguised?

Doug Stauffer can be reached by mail, website, phone or email as follows:

Mail: Dr. Douglas D. Stauffer
Key of Knowledge Ministries
P.O. Box 1611
Millbrook, AL 36054

Website: www.McCowenMills.com

Phone: 334-285-6650 (home); 334-221-1611 (cell); 866-344-1611 (toll free for orders)

Email: dougstauffer@rightlydivided.com